WHO AM I?

Perfection Learning

EDITORIAL DIRECTOR	Julie A. Schumacher
SENIOR EDITOR	Terry Ofner
EDITOR	Rebecca Christian
PERMISSIONS	Laura Pieper
REVIEWERS	Claudia Katz
	Sue Ann Kuby

DESIGN AND PHOTO RESEARCH   William Seabright and Associates, Wilmette, Illinois

COVER ART   SEATED GIRL WITH DOG 1944 Milton Avery

ACKNOWLEDGMENTS
   Text of "Almost Ready" from *Slow Dance Heart Break Blues* by Arnold Adoff. Text copyright© 1995 by Arnold Adoff. Reprinted by permission of Lothrop, Lee and Shepard Books, a division of William Morrow and Company, Inc.
   "Be-ers and Doers" from *The Leaving and Other Stories* by Budge Wilson. Copyright © 1990 by Budge Wilson, compilation. Used by permission of Philomel Books, a division of Penguin Putnam, Inc. Additional permission granted by Stoddart Publishing Co. Ltd., 34 Lesmill Road, Toronto, Ontario, Canada M3B 2T6.
   Text of "The Birthday Box" by Jane Yolen, from *Birthday Surprises: Ten Great Stories to Unwrap*, edited by Johanna Hurwitz. Text copyright © 1995 by Jane Yolen. Reprinted by permission of Morrow Junior Books, a division of William Morrow and Company, Inc.
   "Born Worker" from *Petty Crimes* by Gary Soto, copyright © 1998 by Gary Soto, reprinted by permission of Harcourt, Inc.
   "The Changeling" by Judith Ortíz Cofer. Reprinted from the *Prairie Schooner* by permission of the University of Nebraska Press. Copyright © 1992 by the University of Nebraska Press.
   "Dolly's False Legacy" by Ian Wilmut, from *Time* magazine, January 11, 1999. Copyright © 1999 Time, Inc. Reprinted by permission.   CONTINUED ON PAGE 144

Who's the Real You?

The question above is the *essential question* that you will consider as you read this book. The literature, activities, and organization of the book will lead you to think critically about this question and to develop a deeper understanding of who you are.

To help you shape your answer to the broad essential question, you will read and respond to four sections, or clusters. Each cluster addresses a specific question and thinking skill.

CLUSTER ONE How do I find out who I am? **DEFINE**

CLUSTER TWO Where do I fit? **ANALYZE**

CLUSTER THREE What do I believe? **EVALUATE**

CLUSTER FOUR Thinking on your own **SYNTHESIZE**

Notice that the final cluster asks you to think independently about your answer to the essential question—*Who's the real you?*

WHO AM I?

ALMOST READY:

I	as		as	as
am	this		soon	soon
going	cool		as	as
to	and		I	I
her	in-		find	find
birth-	control		my	my
day	young		new	hip
party	dude:		shirt,	shoes,

as   as
soon   soon
as   as
I   I
find   find
my   my
deep   right
voice,   mask.

Arnold Adoff

TABLE OF CONTENTS

CLUSTER FOUR THINKING ON YOUR OWN

Thinking Skill SYNTHESIZING

Living the Examined Life: An Inside Job

Imagine that you wake up one morning with no memory. It's called total amnesia. You have no idea whether the house you find yourself in is your own. You don't know whether anything in it belongs to you. People you meet seem to know you, and they call you by a name you can't recall ever having heard. Much to their alarm, you have no idea who they are. You have no memory of the life you have lived or are supposed to be living now.

But perhaps the situation is not as dire as it seems. You soon find yourself surrounded by family members, friends, and acquaintances who know exactly who you are. They can tell you where you go to school or what you do for a living. They can tell you all about your likes and dislikes, your weaknesses and strengths, your faults and virtues, your hopes and fears.

You might start living out this identity that other people have told you about. And pretty soon, your life might even seem quite normal.

Then again, maybe you don't want others to make all these decisions for you. Perhaps you even find your forgetfulness oddly liberating. When looking through your wardrobe, you might ask, "What am I doing with these clothes? Do I have to wear them, just because people say that I like them?" And when encountering someone you've been told that you don't get along with, you might wonder, "What's wrong with this person, really? Do we have to be enemies just because people say that we are?" By asking such questions, you begin to take charge of re-creating your own identity.

What does "identity" mean, exactly? Perhaps it can be defined as the answer to the question, "Who are you?" You might identify yourself as the member of some group—a family, an ethnicity, a race, a religion, a club. Perhaps you identify yourself by some skill or talent—as a writer, an artist, an athlete, a musician, or a mathematician. Or perhaps you identify yourself according to places you've been and experiences you've had.

The trouble is, it can be all too easy to let other people define our identities—even if we're not suffering from amnesia. The world seems to be full of experts, and it is often hard not to believe them—even when they offer the most negative messages. Do you have enough money? Are you as beautiful or handsome as you ought to be? Do you own the right car? Do you live in the right neighborhood? The mass media—like some people— often tell you, "No."

It is important to question such messages from time to time, to look at your life from your *own* perspective— a perspective which is easy to lose in a world full of outside experts. As the amnesia scenario suggests, creating a durable identity is an "inside job," and should not be left to others. "The unexamined life is not worth living," said the Greek philosopher Socrates. He might have gone further and said that the unexamined life is no life at all.

Concept Vocabulary

You will find the following terms and definitions useful as you read and discuss the selections in this book.

ambivalence a feeling of being torn between two choices

angst a feeling of anxiety or apprehension

autonomy freedom; having control over one's life and destiny

character the distinctive qualities of an individual

confidence faith or belief in oneself

demeanor a person's outward manner

destiny what a person receives in life as distributed by fate or chance (for example, "It was her destiny to be born rich.")

disposition the overall mood of a person

ego the inner self

environment the combination of circumstances and surroundings that influence a person's growth and development

ethics a system of values and morals

extrovert one who looks outward to understand who he or she is; an outgoing person

fate a force that determines outcomes and endings regardless of what individuals do

heredity physical and intellectual qualities that are passed down from generation to generation

identity crisis the confusion and conflict that result when a person isn't sure of the meaning and purpose of life

introvert one who looks inward to understand who he or she is; a shy person

I.Q. an abbreviation for Intelligence Quotient, determined through an intelligence test

morals feelings and judgments about right and wrong that guide a person's behavior

narcissism excessive love of oneself

optimist a person who tends to see the good in things

personality the ways of acting, thinking, and feeling that taken together make a person unique

pessimist a person who tends to see the bad in things

self-absorption a narrow focus on one's own thoughts, activities, or interests

will strong desires or wishes that direct people to take or avoid certain actions

CLUSTER ONE

How Do I Find Out Who I Am?

Thinking Skill DEFINING

Remember Me

VIVIAN VANDE VELDE

I find myself kneeling on the dusty road, doubled over as if in pain—though I remember no pain.

Before me stands a woman, dressed all in black. Her face is wrinkled and old, her eyes blue green and cold. She says, "Let that be a lesson to you, you arrogant pig." Then she raises her arms and all in an instant is transformed into a crow and flies away.

I try to take notice of her direction, which I feel is probably important, but almost immediately lose the tiny speck of black in the glare of the sun. Also, I'm distracted by the thought that I have no idea who the woman is, or why she should have said such a thing to me.

More alarming, I realize I have no idea who I am.

A young man—that I can tell. I frantically ransack my brain, but no name surfaces. No face, either—my own or anyone else's, except the one I've just seen, the old woman's with the cold eyes. *This is ridiculous,* I think, *I'm . . .*

But even with this running start I can't finish the thought. No name. I can't even think: I'm so-and-so's son. I feel no connection to anyone or anything before fifteen seconds ago.

My clothes are satin and brocade.[1] I have two rings, one on each hand—one is set with two emeralds; the other is simple gold, in the form of a dragon eating its own tail. I also have a gold clasp for my cloak. *So,* I reason, *I'm a wealthy man.* And, it takes no memory but only common

---

1 **brocade:** a luxurious fabric with raised designs

sense to know, wealth means power. But I don't feel powerful, without even having a name.

I look around. The countryside is unfamiliar without being strange. I am on a road, fairly wide and clear. The land is a bit hilly, behind me more so, ahead of me less. Also ahead of me, rising above the tops of the trees, I can make out a distant tower. Much closer is a horse, grazing on the weeds by the edge of the road. I think he must be mine, for he is saddled and bridled, and there is no one else in sight, and what need does a woman who can turn herself into a crow have for a horse?

But I have no name for the horse, any more than I have for myself, and he looks at me warily as I rise to my feet.

"It's all right," I assure him, making soft clucking noises to calm him. "Everything is fine."

Obviously we can both see everything is *not* fine, but he lets me approach, although he watches me with eyes so alarmed the whites show around them.

I can tell that the horse, like the clothing, is expensive. So are the horse's accouterments.[2] The saddle is soft leather, just worn enough to be broken in and comfortable, not old or scuffed. The saddlecloth is expensive material and looks brand-new. There are no saddlebags, nothing to tell me who I am or where I'm from.

"Steady," I tell the horse, and I swing up into the saddle. The action seems natural and familiar. I gather I'm accustomed to riding, but there's no further enlightenment. I face the horse in the direction of the tower, which I hope is a castle. Where I hope someone will recognize me.

I imagine someone—there is no face: I'm imagining, not planning— that someone placing a cool cloth on my head. I imagine this person saying, "The poor dear had a nasty spill from the horse, but he'll be fine in the morning."

But I remember the blue-green eyes of the black-clothed woman, and in my heart I know it's not going to be that simple.

▲   ▲   ▲

The tower does turn out to be part of a castle. The castle overlooks a town. Still, no names come to mind.

I ride through the town gate, and people scurry out of the way of my horse. When I get to the gate of the castle itself, guards standing at either

---

2 **accouterments:** pieces of equipment, such as a bridle and reins

side bow, which might mean they recognize me. Or which might mean my clothes and my horse make me look important enough to warrant polite behavior.

In the courtyard, I dismount and a steward[3] comes and bows. "Good day, sir," he says. "May I announce you?" He gestures for a page to come take the horse.

Somewhat reluctantly, for the horse is my only connection to any past at all, I let go of the reins and watch the boy lead the horse in the direction that must be the stables. "Yes," I tell the senior servant. "Please do."

"Your name, sir?" the steward asks.

I sigh, thinking everything would have been so much simpler if this had turned out to be my home. "Don't you know me?" I ask hopefully. Perhaps he'll take guesses, and one of them will sound familiar.

But the steward just says, apologetically, "I'm afraid your lordship's face is unfamiliar to me." His smile gets just the least bit impatient as he waits.

"I . . ." I say. "I seem to have had a mishap on the road . . ."

"Indeed?" the old servant says, sounding decidedly cooler by now.

"I think I may have been struck on the head," I say, unwilling to share the thought that I seem to have gotten on the wrong side of a woman who can turn herself into a crow.

"How unfortunate," the steward says, his tone bland, but his face disapproving. I can tell, by his face, that people of real quality, such as he is used to dealing with, don't have such things happen to them.

"I was hoping," I admit, "that someone might recognize me."

"I don't," the steward says.

"Perhaps someone else," I suggest.

The steward thinks I am insulting him. "I know everyone who comes and goes at this castle," he tells me.

"But maybe," I insist, "the lord of this castle might know me."

The steward looks me up and down as though I'm a disgrace to my fine clothing. But he doesn't dare turn me away for fear that maybe his lord *would* recognize me, so he says, "The lord and his lady may or may not be in the audience hall this afternoon. You may wait there."

"There was a lady on the road . . ." I say, with a flash of remembrance of hard eyes, of the swish of fabric as arms are raised. . . .

"Not *our* lady," the steward assures me, and turns his back on me.

---

3 **steward:** a person who manages household matters in a large estate

I'm so annoyed by his attitude, I call after him, though I know my presence here is dependent on his goodwill, "Once I regain my identity, you'll apologize for your bad manners."

He looks back scornfully. "Doubtful," he says.

▲   ▲   ▲

All afternoon long I wait with a crowd of other petitioners[4] for the arrival of the castle's lord.

As evening shadows lengthen and the wonderful smells of cooking waft into the audience hall, we are told that the lord will not be seeing us today. Go home. Try again some other day.

I ask to see the steward, but he is not available, either. The servants are very sorry, very polite, but in no time I'm back out in the courtyard, and the castle door shuts in my face.

I find out where the stables are, but my horse is not there. When I admit to the stable master that I'm not a guest at the castle, he tells me that the stables only house the horses of the castle inhabitants and their guests.

"But a boy took my horse away," I protest, "when I first arrived and the steward greeted me."

"Ah," the stable master says, "I know who you are."

My heart starts to beat faster, but he only means that the steward has warned him about me. The horse was originally brought to the stable, he says, but the steward ordered him removed when it was discovered I had no legitimate business at the castle. The horse, the stable master says, is tied up out back behind the smallest stable building, and with that he closes the stable door in my face as firmly as the castle servants closed the castle door in my face.

I am unable to remember who I am or anything else about me, but I am fairly certain I have never had doors shut in my face before.

Going to the back of the building, I find my horse tied to a post, looking disconsolate. His saddle has been removed and is sitting on the ground beside him, but the grooms did not have time to curry[5] him before the steward changed their orders. The horse's healthy coat beneath a layer of road dust shows that he's used to better treatment, and, worse yet, there is no vegetation within reach of his tether.

4 **petitioners:** people who come to ask favors or make requests of those in power

5 **curry:** clean the coat of a horse

"Come on, horse," I say, untying him. The area around the castle is all paving stones and packed dirt, so—carrying the saddle—I lead the horse out through the castle gate, through the winding streets of the town, and out the town gate. The smell of all that fine hay and grain just the other side of the stable wall must have been just as frustrating for him as the smell of the castle supper being prepared was for me.

Beyond the town walls there's grass, and the horse is happy with that. We have to wander farther to find a stream, and we both drink from there.

Distantly we hear a bell ringing, and too late I realize it's the town cur-few. By the time we get back to the wall, the gates have been shut and locked for the night.

I tie the horse's reins to a tree, then put the saddle on the ground to use as a pillow. This does *not* feel natural and familiar, and I have the feeling this is *not* something I've done before. Another unpleasant first for me.

▲   ▲   ▲

The night does not bring back any of my lost memories. I try to convince myself that I imagined the old woman with the blue-green eyes, that I really did get struck on the head, and that eventually my memory is bound to return.

But in my heart I know this is not true. In my heart I know that the woman was there, that she was a witch, and that for some reason she has bespelled me.

In the darkest hours I wonder just how far her spell has worked: Has she destroyed my memories, or do I have no memories because previ-ously I did not exist to *have* memories? I think with alarm of all those stories with witches and frogs. *But she didn't call me a frog,* I console myself; *she called me a pig.* Still, while I cannot remember my name, or my family, or my country, there are certain things I know: I know, for one, there is a certain connection between witches and frogs; I know the difference between north, south, east, and west; I know to be embar-rassed and humiliated by the way the servants have treated me; I know how to walk on two legs, and that feels natural to me, as does riding a horse and sleeping—if I could—indoors. But anything personal, anything that could lead me to who I am, is gone. And my only hope is that the unknown lord of this unknown castle in this unknown land will somehow miraculously know me.

In the morning, when the town gates open, I pick what grass and leaves I can feel out of my hair and once again approach the castle.

There's nothing I can do about the grass stains on my clothes. I use the saddlecloth to rub the horse down, and the horse gives me a look that says he's used to *much* better.

I find the steward again, looking more disapproving than before. Perhaps it's the grass stains. Perhaps it's the horse trailing behind me, as far as the reins will let him get so that it appears even *he* doesn't want to be associated with me. Perhaps the steward is worried that I plan to bring the horse with me into the audience hall.

When I ask the steward what the chances are of seeing the lord today, he snorts and says it's Sunday. No audiences on Sunday.

By now I'm so hungry I think: *If the horse gives me any trouble, I'll eat him.* But I know I won't. He may well be my only way to get home.

I find one of the young boys who helps in the stables. First I throw myself on his mercy, but he's pitiless. Then I offer him my ring with the emeralds. One of the things I have no memory of, no sense for, is money. Either I've never had money, or—more likely—I've never not had enough money. I can tell, though, by the glint in the young page's eyes, what a good bargain he's struck. A gold ring with two emeralds for a stall big enough for my horse and—since I have no better choice—myself to stay in until after I've been seen by the lord of the castle. The ring pays for oats and water for the horse, what food the boy can smuggle from the kitchen for me, the use of a currycomb[6] so I can groom the horse, and the boy's secrecy, because I suspect if the steward or the stable master knew, they'd throw us right out.

▲   ▲   ▲

True to his word, the boy keeps me fed with hard cheese and harder bread. This diet does nothing to improve my memory.

After three days the lord finally comes to the audience hall to speak to the petitioners, but there isn't time for him to deal with each of us, and he leaves without seeing me.

The fourth day the lord returns. I realize I'm getting more and more disreputable-looking as I sleep in my clothes, and straw gets ground into my hair, and I pick up the scent of the stables. The servants must be getting alarmed by my continuing presence, for as the lord starts to leave, once again without glancing at me, I see the steward whisper to him. The lord looks up, over the heads of the bowing crowd, and directly at me.

6 **currycomb:** a comb with metal teeth or notched edges

I take a step forward.

The lord leans down to whisper to the steward, shaking his head.

He doesn't know me.

After all this, he doesn't know me.

The lord leaves, the crowd disperses, and the steward comes up to me and smirks, "Ready for your apology?"

He has two younger, burlier servants with him, and they take hold of my arms and fling me out the door.

When I pick myself up, I find my young stable boy watching me. He's holding on to the reins of my horse, and my saddle is flung over the horse's back, though it's not fastened. The boy says, "The stable master found your horse and says you have to leave."

As I take the reins, the boy whispers to me, "For your other ring, I could find another place for you."

I shake my head, knowing I cannot afford his prices.

Heading for the castle gate, I pass the stable master. "It's a good horse, though," he calls out to me. "Are you willing to sell him?"

I shake my head, for the horse is my ride home.

I go out through the castle gate and into the town itself. But I stop short of leaving the town. What should I do? I know I'm lost; but when someone is lost, it's best to stay in one place, lest you accidentally elude anyone searching for you.

Is there anyone searching for me?

I could go from town to town, one step ahead of my would-be res-cuers. And quickly run through all my possessions and be no better off. I decide to stay in this town and hope that there is someone missing me, trying to find me.

Looking from the horse and his saddle to my dragon ring, to the gold sunburst pin that holds my cloak, I notice how shabby my once-fine clothes are beginning to appear. They won't last long, so they're what I'll start with. I begin to search for someone who'll buy the clothes off my back—trade sturdiness for finery and hopefully give me a few extra coins in the bargain so I can eat.

▲ ▲ ▲

With the money I get for trading my clothes and selling my pin, I can afford a week's meals and lodgings for myself and a stall for my horse in the stable of a small inn. Every day I take the horse out to graze on the grass outside the town walls, so I don't have to use up my small amount of money to buy food for him.

I go around the town, talking to people, hungry for names. Nothing sounds familiar. Nobody looks familiar to me. And I look familiar to no one.

The dragon emblem on my ring seems to be just a decoration—it means nothing to anyone. So, after the week, I offer the ring to the owner of the inn. He says it will buy me two more weeks' lodging. I bargain with him. I say: "Three weeks' worth of food, and I'll stay in the stable with the horse."

The innkeeper is not pleased with the arrangement, but finally he agrees. *I'm* not happy with the arrangement, for the stalls are much smaller than at the castle's stables, and I'll be lucky if I don't get stepped on. Still, I'm assuming that in three weeks I'm bound to remember or find out *some*thing about my past.

But after three weeks I have to approach the innkeeper with yet another bargain. "I'll work for my keep," I offer, "mine and the horse's."

The innkeeper lifts up my hand, which is soft and white compared to his. "Never done a day's work in your life," he snorts.

I don't remember, one way or the other, but my hands say he is right.

"I can learn," I tell him.

The innkeeper raises his eyes to the heavens and shakes his head, but he agrees.

My job is to muck out[7] the stable twice every day. In addition, I have to keep the inn clean, too, the common room and the guest rooms. My hands are blistered and my muscles are sore, but I get to eat all the leftovers I can scrape from customers' plates.

Unfortunately, all this work leaves little time for taking my horse out to graze, and meanwhile the weather is beginning to turn colder. Soon there will be no foraging. First I sell the saddle, telling myself that once I find out where home is I can ride there without a saddle. With the money I get from selling it, I buy enough oats to make the horse happy again. For a time.

But then that runs out, and I see he's getting skinnier and skinnier. Eventually I realize I have to sell him soon, or the castle's stable master won't want him.

"I'm sorry, horse," I whisper. I still don't remember his name, and I have no way of knowing how fond of him I was before. Now he is the

---

7 **muck out:** clean manure from

only thing I have left to connect me to the furthest back I can remember: the day on the road with the blue-green-eyed witch.

The stable master buys the horse, with much grumbling and shaking of his head over the horse's sad state. After all we've been through together—maybe *because* of all we've been through—the horse doesn't look sorry to leave me.

As I walk through the town, I give one of my coins to the man with the withered hand who stands on the same street corner every day, begging. It isn't that I have money to spare, but I recognize that this may well be where I end up next.

At the inn the innkeeper tells me that he's sorry—I've been a better worker than he ever imagined—but his nephew has arrived from the country, looking for a job, and the innkeeper has given him mine.

It's been so long since I've been clean, or comfortable, or well fed, I'm desperate enough to be willing to spend some of my money from the sale of my horse to take a room. But when I reach into my pocket, I find nothing there but a hole.

I leave, so that the innkeeper doesn't have to throw me out, the way the castle steward threw me out.

I walk down the street, wondering if I should beg my coin back from the beggar. From behind me, I hear the clatter of horses' hooves on the street. I press against the wall to get out of the way—the lord and lady of the castle and their friends are always tearing through the streets on their fast mounts,[8] careless of the poor folk who have to scurry out of their way.

The riders, two men, have to slow down to take the corner. I look to see if either of the horses is mine, but neither is. I keep walking, the only way to stay warm, but one of the men pulls his horse to a stop; and the second man stops, also, to avoid colliding with him.

"Your Highness?" a voice says.

I look up and around, and it's the first man, and he's looking at me.

"Is it you?" he asks in sick amazement.

"I don't know," I have to admit. "Is it?"

He leaps from his horse for a closer look, then practically kneels, he bows so low.

"Our long-lost prince, found at last," he proclaims to any of the town's inhabitants who might be wondering. He whips off his cloak and puts it

---

8 **mounts:** saddle horses

around me. "Oh, well met,⁹ sir," he exclaims with such joy it nearly breaks my heart.

He orders the younger man with him to get off his horse. "Help His Highness up," he says, "and you walk along behind."

Belatedly the younger man scrambles off his horse, and he actually does kneel on the cobblestones.

"How far to home?" I ask.

"Two weeks' journey," the older man tells me.

I know how sore my feet have been since I sold my fine boots with the rest of my clothing, and I can't subject this poor young squire to walking for two weeks. "We can ride together," I say, which makes his eyes go wide in amazement.

And so we do.

I learn my name, which does not sound familiar, and I learn that I have a father and mother who have been frantic concerning my whereabouts, and there is a princess to whom I am betrothed¹⁰—foreign born but lovely, I'm assured—and none of their names sound familiar, either. And when we finally reach my ancestral lands, nothing *looks* familiar.

The man who found me—one of many such searchers, he informs me—sends word ahead that I have been found, but that my memory has been lost. We enter the courtyard to my own castle—which looks less familiar to me than the castle in the town where I stayed. I return to the sound of trumpets blaring and men cheering and maidens throwing flower petals out the windows to greet me.

A gray-bearded man and a plump woman are standing by the fountain, and before the horses even stop, the woman is rushing forward, crying out, "Oh, my poor, sweet baby."

"Mother," I say, which seems a fairly safe guess, and she throws her arms around me, then turns to the crowd and says, triumphantly, defiantly, "See? He *does* remember."

But I don't.

I have to take other people's word for who I know, and who I like, and what I did as a boy, and what my interests are, and that I love my parents, and that I'm happy with my betrothal to the princess.

They tell me I'm calmer than I ever was before, and more patient, and kinder. Which sound like compliments, until I think about it. When I point

---

9 **well met:** an old-fashioned term used as an enthusiastic greeting

10 **betrothed:** engaged to be married

this out, everybody laughs and says, *No, no, but we mean it—we loved you before, but you're gentler and more considerate since your adventure.*

Whatever my adventure was.

Which is the one thing none of them knows, either.

And *nothing* seems familiar.

Except, sometimes, when I look at the princess I'm to marry, I find her looking at me with an expression that's almost familiar, watching carefully, appraisingly, and her eyes are cool blue green, and that's something I don't want to think about at all. ∾

On Being Seventeen, Bright, and Unable to Read

DAVID RAYMOND

One day a substitute teacher picked me to read aloud from the text-book. When I told her, "No, thank you," she came unhinged. She thought I was acting smart and told me so. I kept calm, and that got her madder and madder. We must have spent 10 minutes trying to solve the problem, and finally she got so red in the face I thought she'd blow up. She told me she'd see me after class.

Maybe someone like me was a new thing for that teacher. But she wasn't new to me. I've been through scenes like that all my life. You see, even though I'm 17 and a junior in high school, I can't read because I have dyslexia.[1] I'm told I read "at a fourth-grade level," but from where I sit, that's not reading. You can't know what that means unless you've been there. It's not easy to tell how it feels when you can't read your homework assignments or the newspaper or a menu in a restaurant or even notes from your own friends.

My family began to suspect I was having problems almost from the first day I started school. My father says my early years in school were the worst years of his life. They weren't so good for me, either. As I look back on it now, I can't find the words to express how bad it really was. I wanted to die. I'd come home from school screaming, "I'm dumb. I'm dumb—I wish I were dead!"

1 **dyslexia:** a reading disability

I guess I couldn't read anything at all then—not even my own name—and they tell me I didn't talk as good as other kids. But what I remember about those days is that I couldn't throw a ball where it was supposed to go, I couldn't learn to swim, and I wouldn't learn to ride a bike, because no matter what anyone told me, I knew I'd fail.

Sometimes my teachers would try to be encouraging. When I couldn't read the words on the board, they'd say, "Come on, David, you know that word." Only I didn't. And it was embarrassing. I just felt dumb. And dumb was how the kids treated me. They'd make fun of me every chance they got, asking me to spell *cat* or something like that. Even if I knew how to spell it, I wouldn't; they'd only give me another word. Anyway, it was awful, because more than anything I wanted friends. On my birthday when I blew out the candles I didn't wish I could learn to read; what I wished for was that the kids would like me.

With the bad reports coming from school, and with me moaning about wanting to die and how everybody hated me, my parents began looking for help. That's when the testing started. The school tested me, the child-guidance center tested me, private psychiatrists tested me. Everybody knew something was wrong—especially me.

It didn't help much when they stuck a fancy name onto it. I couldn't pronounce it then—I was only in second grade—and I was ashamed to talk about it. Now it rolls off my tongue, because I've been living with it for a lot of years—dyslexia.

Elementary School All through elementary school it wasn't easy. I was always having to do things that were "different," things the other kids didn't have to do. I had to go to a child psychiatrist, for instance.

One summer my family forced me to go to a camp for children with reading problems. I hated the idea, but the camp turned out pretty good, and I had a good time. I met a lot of kids who couldn't read and somehow that helped. The director of the camp said I had a higher IQ than 90 percent of the population. I didn't believe him.

About the worst thing I had to do in fifth and sixth grade was go to a special education class in another school in our town. A bus picked me up, and I didn't like that at all. The bus also picked up emotionally disturbed kids and retarded kids. It was like going to a school for the retarded. I always worried that someone I knew would see me on that bus. It was a relief to go to the regular junior high school.

Junior High School Life began to change a little for me, then, because I began to feel better about myself. I found the teachers cared; they had meetings about me and I worked harder for them for a while. I began to work on the potter's wheel, making vases and pots that the teachers said were pretty good. Also, I got a letter for being on the track team. I could always run pretty fast.

High School At high school the teachers are good and everyone is trying to help me. I've gotten honors some marking periods, and I've won a letter on the cross-country team. Next quarter I think the school might hold a show of my pottery. I've got some friends. But there are still some embarrassing times. For instance, every time there is writing in the class, I get up and go to the special education room. Kids ask me where I go all the time. Sometimes I say, "to Mars."

Homework is a real problem. During free periods in school I go into the special ed room, and staff members read assignments to me. When I get home, my mother reads to me. Sometimes she reads an assignment into a tape recorder, and then I go into my room and listen to it. If we have a novel or something like that to read, she reads it out loud to me. Then I sit down with her and we do the assignment. She'll write, while I talk my answers to her. Lately I've taken to dictating into a tape recorder, and then someone—my father, a private tutor, or my mother—types up what I've dictated. Whatever homework I do takes someone else's time, too. That makes me feel bad.

We had a big meeting in school the other day—eight of us, four from the guidance department, my private tutor, my parents and me. The subject was me. I said I wanted to go to college, and they told me about colleges that have facilities and staff to handle people like me. That's nice to hear.

As for what happens after college, I don't know and I'm worried about that. How can I make a living if I can't read? Who will hire me? How will I fill out the application form? The only thing that gives me any courage is the fact that I've learned about well-known people who couldn't read or had other problems and still made it. Like Albert Einstein, who didn't talk until he was 4 and flunked math. Like Leonardo da Vinci, who everyone seems to think had dyslexia.

I've told this story because maybe some teacher will read it and go easy on a kid in the classroom who has what I've got. Or, maybe some parent will stop nagging his kid and stop calling him lazy. Maybe he's not lazy or dumb. Maybe he just can't read and doesn't know what's wrong. Maybe he's scared, like I was. ❧

Editor's Note:

This essay first appeared in The New York Times *in 1976. Raymond later attended college and graduated cum laude, with honors.*

YOUR BODY IS YOUR ID

HANK SCHLESINGER

Forget your ID card. PIN numbers and passwords have become strictly passé. These and other old-fashioned methods of proving your identity are no longer up to snuff in an age in which personal information can be easily pilfered by computer-savvy renegades[1] and pranksters.

Instead, get ready for a world in which your body—or more accurately, certain parts of it—is proof that you are who you claim to be. This technique is called biometrics, defined as the automated identification of an individual based on unique physiological characteristics.

The most familiar biometric technique is fingerprinting, but whipping out a magnifying glass and then checking a print against a database of potential matches can lead to long lines at security checkpoints. Now, computers can make matches in seconds, sparking new varieties of biometric identification with their ever-increasing processing power. Identification databases can be searched to match facial features, the geometry of your hand, your voice, and even your iris.

Virtually all biometric devices employ the same general principle. First, a sample is collected. That sample, whether it be an image of a face or a digital representation[2] of a voice, is then processed through a feature-extraction system that uses an algorithm[3] to assign it a code based on its unique characteristics. This code is stored in a database until you present

---

1 **renegades:** deserters, in this case from a company or an organization

2 **digital representation:** a copy of something readable by a device such as a computer

3 **algorithm:** a step-by-step procedure

yourself for identification, at which time a feature-matching algorithm makes a match between you and the code stored in the database.

Biometric identification systems are proving to be remarkably accurate and fast. A Mr. Payroll check-cashing machine that relies on face recognition is already processing thousands of transactions per day at locations throughout the South, for example. And multiple biometric systems can be used together to bring accuracy near the 100 percent level.

So the next time someone asks you for identification, he may want to look you in the eye—just to make sure you're not just another pretty face.

Eye Technology The iris of your eye consists of a complex fibrous tissue that stretches as pupil diameter varies. Random processes that occur before birth create detail in the texture. No iris patterns, even those between the right and left eye of the same person, are identical.

Face Technology With face recognition, the sum of the parts is greater than the whole. Rather than take a picture of the entire face, these systems analyze some 50 points around the nose, mouth, eyebrows, jaw, and other facial areas where the curvature of bone changes. These points are arranged to create a pattern. The computer is programmed to compensate for slight shifts in facial expression.

Voice Technology Of all the biometric systems, voice identification is the trickiest and least accurate. The human voice, after all, has a behavioral component: It tends to change with shifts in mood (never mind the influence of a cold or other illness).

Finger Technology Fingerprinting is migrating away from law enforcement into such security applications as computer network access. Some systems, like the Bio-mouse from American Biometric, are based on simple scanners, but the technology continues to become more complex and automated.

Hand Technology In hand geometry systems, the size and shape of individual fingers and knuckles as well as the overall size of the hand is measured in three dimensions according to a proprietary[4] formula. ∾

4 **proprietary:** privately owned

For more about biometric identification, see the diagram on the next two pages. ➡

EYE TECHNOLOGY

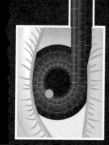

A picture of your iris is translated into a string of digital code using a mathematical technique called wavelet analysis. An iris has about 266 measurable characteristics, as opposed to about 40 for fingerprints; the characteristics can now be identified by a camera positioned as far as 3 feet away. Variations among irises are so many that the system can mismatch a third of the information stored as iris code and still make a positive identification. Iris scans are the most secure of all biometric systems, ahead of even fingerprinting.

FACE TECHNOLOGY

Highly sophisticated systems can automatically sense a person's presence, follow the movement of his head, and compare the image to a database even when the lighting conditions in the two pictures are different. A stereo-camera configuration foils anyone sneaky enough to try placing a photo in front of the lens. Twins still present a problem, however, as do people who subsequently grow beards or gain weight.

VOICE TECHNOLOGY

Voice systems plot the frequencies your voice produces every 1/100th of a second. These frequency graphs are placed together side by side to produce a bumpy three-dimensional image called a waterfall that represents the sound of your voice over a full second. Transitions between phonemes, the smallest units of speech, are characterized by a line graph of curved and straight arrows.

HAND TECHNOLOGY

When you press your hand against a scanner, the image is compared against a database of authorized users. Though quickly obtained, a hand configuration is not as accurate an identifier as an iris, fingerprint, or face—even though scanners are sophisticated enough not to be thrown off by a ring, for example. That's why one system under development for border crossings would link hand geometry and credit card numbers for closer matches to a database of undesirable visitors.

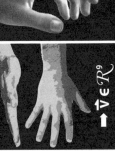

FINGER TECHNOLOGY

The Finger-Chip made by Thomson-CSF Semiconductors Specifique utilizes thermal imaging. A person sweeps a finger over the surface of a computer chip that reads the heat signature of the finger to reconstruct a pattern. Similarly, a chip made by Veridicom constructs a fingerprint image by using thousands of sensing capacitors to pick up electrical charges emitted by the finger.

The Changeling

JUDITH ORTÍZ COFER

          As a young girl
vying for my father's attention,
I invented a game that made him look up
from his reading and shake his head
as if both baffled and amused.

In my brother's closet, I'd change
into his dungarees[1]—the rough material
molding me into boy-shape; hide
my long hair under an army helmet
he'd been given by Father, and emerge
transformed into the legendary Ché[2]
of grown-up talk.

Strutting around the room,
I'd tell of life in the mountains,
of carnage and rivers of blood,
and of manly feasts with rum and music
to celebrate victories *para la libertad.*[3]
He would listen with a smile
to my tales of battles and brotherhood
until Mother called us to dinner.

She was not amused
by my transformations, sternly forbidding me
from sitting down with them as a man.
She'd order me back to the dark cubicle
that smelled of adventure, to shed
my costume, to braid my hair furiously
with blind hands, and to return invisible,
as myself,
to the real world of her kitchen.

1 **dungarees:** trousers made of heavy, durable material
2 **Ché:** Ernesto (Ché) Guevara: Argentine-born revolutionary leader
3 *para la libertad :* for freedom

Transformación

TRANSLATED FROM THE ENGLISH BY JOHANNA VEGA

Cuando era pequeña,
compitiendo por la atención de mi padre,
inventé un juego que lo hacía levantar la vista
de lo que léia y mover la cabeza
como si estuviera a la vez sorprendido y divertido.

En el armario de mi hermano, me ponía
sus pantalones—el áspero material hacía
que mi cuerpo pareciera el de un chico; escondía
mi pelo largo en el casco
que le había regalado papá y salía
transformada en el legendario Ché
de las conversaciones adultas.

Pavoneándome en el cuarto,
hablaba de la vida en las montañas,
de las mantanzas y los ríos de sangre,
y de los banquetes masculinos con ron y mantanzas música
para celebrar los triunfos para la libertad.
Con una sonrisa él escuchaba
mis cuentos de batallas y fraternidad
hasta que mamá nos llamaba a cenar.

A ella no le divertían
mis transformaciones, prohibiéndome severamente
que me sentara con ellos como hombre.
Me ordenaba que volviera al cubículo
que olía a aventuras para quitarme
el disfraz, para trenzarme el pelo furiosamente
con manos ciegas y que regresara invisible,
como yo misma,
al mundo real de su cocina.

Be-ers and Doers

BUDGE WILSON

Mom was a little narrow wisp of a woman. You wouldn't have thought to look at her that she could move a card table; even for me it was sometimes hard to believe the ease with which she could shove around an entire family. Often I tried to explain her to myself. She had been brought up on the South Shore of Nova Scotia.[1] I wondered sometimes if the scenery down there had rubbed off on her—all those granite rocks and fogs and screeching gulls, the slow, laboring springs, and the quick, grudging summers. And then the winters—grayer than doom, and endless.

I was the oldest. I was around that house for five years before Maudie came along. They were peaceful, those five years, and even now it's easy to remember how everything seemed calm and simple. But now I know why. I was a conformist and malleable[2] as early as three years old; I didn't buck the system. If Mom said, "Hurry, Adelaide!" If she said to me, at five, "Fold that laundry, now, Adie, and don't let no grass grow under your feet," I folded it fast. So there were very few battles at first, and no major wars.

Dad, now, he was peaceful just by nature. If a tornado had come whirling in the front door and lifted the roof clear off its hinges, he probably would have just scratched the back of his neck and said, with a kind of slow surprise, "Well! Oho! Just think o'that!" He had been born in the Annapolis Valley,[3] where the hills are round and gentle, and the summers sunlit and very warm.

1 **Nova Scotia:** a province in SE Canada
2 **malleable:** willing to be molded
3 **Annapolis Valley:** an area in western Nova Scotia

"Look at your father!" Mom would say to us later. "He thinks that all he's gotta do is *be*. Well, bein' ain't good enough. You gotta *do*, too. Me, I'm a doer." All the time she was talking, she'd be knitting up a storm, or mixing dough, or pushing a mop—hands forever and ever on the move.

Although Mom was fond of pointing out to us the things our father didn't do, he must have been doing something. Our farm was in the most fertile part of the valley, and it's true that we had the kind of soil that seemed to make things grow all of their own accord. Those beets and carrots and potatoes just came pushing up into the sunshine with an effortless grace, and they kept us well fed, with plenty left over to sell. But there was weeding and harvesting to do, and all those ten cows to milk—not to mention the thirty apple trees in our orchard to be cared for. I think maybe he just did his work so slowly and quietly that she found it hard to believe he was doing anything at all. Besides, on the South Shore, nothing ever grew without a struggle. And when Dad was through all his chores, or in between times, he liked to just sit on our old porch swing and watch the spring unfold or the summer blossom. And in the fall, he sat there smiling, admiring the rows of vegetables, the giant sunflowers, the golden leaves gathering in the trees of North Mountain.

Maudie wasn't Maudie for the reasons a person is a Ginny or a Gertie or a Susie. She wasn't called Maudie because she was cute. She got that name because if you've got a terrible name like Maud, you have to do something to rescue it. She was called after Mom's aunt Maud, who was a miser and had the whole Bank of Nova Scotia under her mattress. But she was a crabby old thing who just sat around living on her dead husband's stocks and bonds. A be-er, not a doer. Mom really scorned Aunt Maud and hated her name, but she had high hopes that our family would sometime cash in on that gold mine under the mattress. She hadn't counted on Aunt Maud going to Florida one winter and leaving her house in the care of a dear old friend. The dear old friend emptied the contents of the mattress, located Aunt Maud's three diamond rings, and took off for Mexico, leaving the pipes to freeze and the cat to die of starvation. After that, old Aunt Maud couldn't have cared less if everybody in the whole district had been named after her. She was that bitter.

Maudie was so like Mom that it was just as if she'd been cut out with a cookie cutter from the same dough. Raced around at top speed all through her growing-up time, full of projects and sports and hobbies and gossip and nerves. And mad at everyone who sang a different tune.

But this story's not about Maudie. I guess you could say it's mostly about Albert.

Albert was the baby. I was eight years old when he was born, and I often felt like he was my own child. He was special to all of us, I guess, except maybe to Maudie, and when Mom saw him for the first time, I watched a slow soft tenderness in her face that was a rare thing for any of us to see. I was okay because I was cooperative, and I knew she loved me. Maudie was her clone, and almost like a piece of herself, so they admired one another, although they were too similar to be at peace for very long. But Albert was something different. Right away, I knew she was going to pour into Albert something that didn't reach the rest of us, except in part. As time went on, this scared me. I could see that she'd made up her mind that Albert was going to be a perfect son. That meant, among other things, that he was going to be a fast-moving doer. And even when he was three or four, it wasn't hard for me to know that this wasn't going to be easy. Because Albert was a be-er. *Born* that way.

As the years went by, people around Wilmot used to say, "Just look at that family of Hortons. Mrs. Horton made one child—Maudie. Then there's Adelaide, who's her own self. But Albert, now. Mr. Horton made him all by himself. They're alike as two pine needles."

And just as nice, I could have added. But Mom wasn't either pleased or amused. "You're a bad influence on that boy, Stanley," she'd say to my dad. "How's he gonna get any ambition if all he sees is a father who can spend up to an hour leanin' on his hoe, starin' at the Mountain?" Mom had it all worked out that Albert was going to be a lawyer or a doctor or a Member of Parliament.[4]

My dad didn't argue with her, or at least not in an angry way, "Aw, c'mon now, Dorothy," he might say to her, real slow. "The vegetables are comin' along jest fine. No need to shove them more than necessary. It does a man good to look at them hills. You wanta try it sometime. They tell you things."

"Nothin' *I* need t'hear," she'd huff, and disappear into the house, clattering pans, thumping the mop, scraping the kitchen table across the floor to get at more dust. And Albert would just watch it all, saying not a word, chewing on a piece of grass.

Mom really loved my dad, even though he drove her nearly crazy. Lots more went on than just nagging and complaining. If you looked really

---

4 **Parliament:** the highest legislative body in Canada

hard, you could see that. If it hadn't been for Albert and wanting him to be a four-star son, she mightn't have bothered to make Dad look so useless. Even so, when they sat on the swing together at night, you could feel their closeness. They didn't hold hands or anything. Her hands were always too busy embroidering, crocheting, mending something, or just swatting mosquitoes. But they liked to be together. Personal chemistry, I thought as I grew older, is a mysterious and contrary thing.

One day, Albert brought his report card home from school, and Mom looked at it hard and anxious, eyebrows knotted. "'Albert seems a nice child,'" she read aloud to all of us, more loudly than necessary, "'but his marks could be better. He spends too much time looking out the window, dreaming.'" She paused. No one spoke.

"Leanin' on his hoe," continued Mom testily. "Albert!" she snapped at him. "You pull up your socks by Easter or you're gonna be in deep trouble."

Dad stirred uneasily in his chair. "Aw, Dorothy," he mumbled. "Leave him be. He's a good kid."

"Or could be. *Maybe*," she threw back at him. "What he seems like to me is rock-bottom lazy. He sure is slow-moving, and could be he's slow in the head, too. Dumb."

Albert's eyes flickered at that word, but that's all. He just stood there and watched, eyes level.

"But I love him a lot," continued Mom, "and unlike you, I don't plan t'just sit around and watch him grow dumber. If it's the last thing I do, I'm gonna light a fire under his feet."

Albert was twelve then, and the nagging began to accelerate in earnest.

"How come you got a low mark in your math test?"

"I don't like math. It seems like my head don't want it."

"But do you *work* at it?"

"Well, no. Not much. Can't see no sense in workin' hard at something I'll never use. I can add up our grocery bill. I pass. That's enough."

"Not for me, it ain't," she'd storm back at him. "No baseball practice for you until you get them sums perfect. Ask Maudie t'check them." Maudie used to drum that arithmetic into him night after night. She loved playing schoolteacher, and that's how she eventually ended up. And a cross one.

One thing Albert was good at, though, was English class. By the time he got to high school, he spent almost as much time reading as he did staring into space. His way of speaking changed. He stopped dropping his *g*'s. He said *isn't* instead of *ain't*. His tenses were all neated up. He wasn't putting on airs. I just think that all those people in his books started being more real to him than his own neighbors. He loved animals, too. He made friends with the calves and even the cows. Mutt and Jeff, our two gray cats, slept on his bed every night. Often you could see him out in the fields, talking to our dog, while he was working.

"Always messin' around with animals," complained Mom. "Sometimes I think he's three parts woman and one part child. He's fifteen years old, and last week I caught him bawlin' in the hayloft after we had to shoot that male calf. Couldn't understand why y' can't go on feedin' an animal that'll never produce milk."

"Nothing wrong with liking animals," I argued. I was home for the weekend from my secretarial job in Wolfville.

"Talkin' to dogs and cryin' over cattle is not what I'd call a shortcut to success. And the cats spend so much time with him that they've forgotten why we brought them into the house in the first place. For mice."

"Maybe there's more to life than success or mice," I said. I was twenty-three now, and more interested in Albert than in conformity.

Mom made a "huh" sound through her nose. "Adelaide Horton," she said, "when you're my age, you'll understand more about success and mice than you do now. Or the lack of them." She turned on her heel and went back in the house. "And if you can't see," she said through the screen door, "why I don't want Albert to end up exactly like your father, then you've got even less sense than I thought you had. I don't want any son of mine goin' though life just satisfied to *be*." Then I could hear her banging around in the kitchen.

I looked off the verandah out at the front field, where Dad and Albert were raking up hay for the cattle, slowly, with lots of pauses for talk. All of a sudden they stopped, and Albert pointed up to the sky. It was fall, and four long wedges of geese were flying far above us, casting down their strange muffled cry. The sky was cornflower blue, and the wind was sending white clouds scudding across it. My breath was caught with the beauty of it all, and as I looked at Dad and Albert, they threw away their rakes and lay down flat on their backs, right there in the front pasture, in order to drink in the sky. And after all the geese had passed over, they stayed like that for maybe twenty minutes more.

▲　▲　▲

We were all home for Christmas the year Albert turned eighteen. Maudie was having her Christmas break from teaching, and she was looking skinnier and more tight-lipped than I remembered her. I was there with my husband and my new baby, Jennifer, and Albert was even quieter than usual. But content, I thought. Not making any waves. Mom had intensified her big campaign to have him go to Acadia University in the fall. "Pre-law," she said, "or maybe teacher training. Anyways, you gotta go. A man has to be successful." She avoided my father's eyes. "In the fall," she said. "For sure."

"It's Christmas," said Dad, without anger. "Let's just be happy and forget all them plans for a few days." He was sitting at the kitchen table breaking up the bread slowly, slowly, for the turkey stuffing. He chuckled. "I've decided to be a doer this Christmas."

"And if the doin's bein' done at that speed," she said, taking the bowl from him, "we'll be eatin' Christmas dinner on New Year's Day." She started to break up the bread so quickly that you could hardly focus on her flying fingers.

Christmas came and went. It was a pleasant time. The food was good; Jennifer slept right through dinner and didn't cry all day. We listened to the Queen's Christmas message;[5] we opened presents. Dad gave Mom a ring with a tiny sapphire in it, although she'd asked for a new vacuum cleaner.

"I like this better," she said, and looked as though she might cry.

"We'll get the vacuum cleaner in January," he said, "That's no kind of gift to get for Christmas. It's a work thing."

She looked as if she might say something, but she didn't.

▲   ▲   ▲

It was on December 26th that it happened. That was the day of the fire.

It was a lazy day. We all got up late, except me, of course, who had to feed the baby at two and at six. But when we were all up, we just sort of

5 **Queen's Chrismas message:** a holiday greeting from the British queen, to whom Canada is loyal as a member of the Commonwealth of Nations

lazed around in our dressing gowns, drinking coffee, admiring one anothers' presents, talking about old times, singing a carol or two around the old organ. Dad had that look on him that he used to get when all his children were in his house at the same time. Like he was in temporary possession of the best that life had to offer. Even Mom was softened up, and she sat by the grate fire and talked a bit, although there was still a lot of jumping up and down and rushing out to the kitchen to check the stove or cut up vegetables. Me, I think that on the day after Christmas you should just eat up leftovers and enjoy a slow state of collapse. But you can't blame a person for feeding you. It's handy to have a Martha or two around a house that's already equipped with three Marys.[6] Albert was the best one to watch, though. To me, anyway. He was sitting on the floor in his striped pajamas, holding Jennifer, rocking her, and singing songs to her in a low, crooning voice. Tender, I thought, the way I like a man to be.

Albert had just put the baby back in her carriage when a giant spark flew out of the fireplace. It hit the old nylon carpet like an incendiary[7] bomb, and the rug burst into flames. Mom started waving an old afghan over it, as though she was blowing out a match, but all she was doing was fanning the fire.

While most of us stood there in immovable fear, Albert had already grabbed Jennifer, carriage and all, and rushed out to the barn with her. He was back in a flash, just in time to see Maudie's dressing gown catch fire. He pushed her down on the floor and lay on top of her to smother the flames, and then he was up on his feet again, taking charge.

6 **Martha...Marys:** In the Bible, Martha bustled with household tasks while Mary sat at the feet of Jesus; the two have come to symbolize contrasting approaches to life, the practical and the philosophical.

7 **incendiary:** fire-starting

"Those four buckets in the summer kitchen!" he yelled. "Start filling them!" He pointed to Mom and Dad, who obeyed him like he was a general and they were the privates. To my husband he roared, "Get out to th' barn and keep that baby warm!"

"And you!" He pointed to me. "Call the fire department. It's 825-3131." In the meantime, the smoke was starting to fill the room and we were all coughing. Little spits of fire were crawling up the curtains, and Maudie was just standing there, shrieking.

Before Mom and Dad got back with the water, Albert was out in the back bedroom hauling up the carpet. Racing in with it over his shoulder, he bellowed, "Get out o' the way!" and we all moved. Then he slapped the carpet over the flames on the floor, and the fire just died without so much as a protest. Next he grabbed one of the big cushions off the sofa, and chased around after the little lapping flames on curtains and chairs and table runners, smothering them. When Mom and Dad appeared with a bucket in each hand, he shouted, "Stop! Don't use that stuff! No need t'have water damage too!"

Then Albert was suddenly still, hands hanging at his sides with the fingers spread. He smiled shyly.

"It's out," he said.

I rushed up and hugged him, wailing like a baby, loving him, thanking him. For protecting Jennifer—from smoke, from fire, from cold, from heaven knows what. Everyone opened windows and doors, and before too long, even the smoke was gone. It smelled pretty awful, but no one cared.

When we all gathered again in the parlor to clear up the mess, and Jennifer was back in my bedroom asleep, Mom stood up and looked at Albert, her eyes ablaze with admiration—and with something else I couldn't put my finger on.

"Albert!" she breathed. "We all thank you! You've saved the house, the baby, all of us, even our Christmas presents. I'm proud, proud, *proud* of you."

Albert just stood there, smiling quietly, but very pale. His hands were getting red and sort of puckered looking.

Mom took a deep breath. "And *that,*" she went on, "is what I've been looking for, all of your life. Some sort of a sign that you were one hundred percent alive. And now we all know you are. Maybe even a lick more alive than the rest of us. So!" She folded her arms, and her eyes bored into him. "I'll have no more excuses from you now. No one who can put out a house fire single-handed and rescue a niece and a sister and organize us all into a fire brigade[8] is gonna sit around for the rest of his life gatherin' dust. No siree! Or leanin' against no hoe. Why, you even had the fire department number tucked away in your head. Just imagine what you're gonna be able to do with them kind o' brains! I'll never, never rest until I see you educated and successful. Doin' what you was meant to do. I'm just proud of you, Albert. So terrible proud!"

Members of the fire department were starting to arrive at the front door, but Albert ignored them. He was white now, like death, and he made a low and terrible sound. He didn't exactly pull his lips back from his teeth and growl, but the result was similar. It was like the sound a dog makes before he leaps for the throat. And what he said was *"You jest leave me be, woman!"*

We'd never heard words like this coming out of Albert, and the parlor was as still as night as we all listened.

"You ain't proud o' me, Mom," he whispered, all his beautiful grammar gone. "Yer jest proud o' what you want me t'be. And I got some news for you. Things I shoulda tole you years gone by. *I ain't gonna be what you want.*" His voice was starting to quaver now, and he was trembling all over. *"I'm gonna be me.* And it seems like if that's ever gonna happen, it'll have t'be in some other place. And I plan t'do somethin' about that before the day is out."

Then he shut his eyes and fainted right down onto the charred carpet. The firemen carted him off to the hospital, where he was treated for shock and second-degree burns. He was there for three weeks.

▲ ▲ ▲

My dad died of a stroke when he was sixty-six. "Not enough exercise," said Mom, after she'd got over the worst part of her grief. "Too much sittin' around watchin' the lilacs grow. No way for his blood to circulate good." Me, I ask myself if he just piled up his silent tensions until he burst wide open. Maybe he wasn't all that calm and peaceful after all. Could be he was just waiting, like Albert, for the moment when it would all come pouring out. Perhaps that wasn't the way it was; but all the same, I wonder.

Mom's still going strong at eighty-eight. Unlike Dad's, her blood must circulate like a racing stream, what with all that rushing around; she continues to move as if she's being chased. She's still knitting and preserving

---

8 **fire brigade:** a group formed to fight fires

and scrubbing and mending and preaching. She'll never get one of those tension diseases like angina[9] or cancer or even arthritis, because she doesn't keep one single thing bottled up inside her for more than five minutes. Out it all comes like air out of a flat tire—with either a hiss or a bang.

Perhaps it wasn't growing up on the South Shore that made Mom the way she is. I live on that coast now, and I've learned that it's more than just gray and stormy. I know about the long sandy beaches and the peace that comes of a clear horizon. I've seen the razzle-dazzle colors of the low-lying scarlet bushes in the fall, blazing against the black of the spruce trees and the bluest sky in the world. I'm familiar with the way one single radiant summer day can make you forget a whole fortnight of fog—like birth after a long labor. You might say that the breakers[10] out on the reefs are angry or full of threats. To me, though, those waves are leaping and dancing, wild with freedom and joyfulness. But I think Mom was in a hurry from the moment she was born. I doubt if she ever stopped long enough to take notice of things like that.

Albert left home as soon as he got out of the hospital. He worked as a stevedore[11] in Halifax for a number of years, and when he got enough money saved, he bought a little run-down house close to Digby, with a view of the Bay of Fundy.[12] He's got a small chunk of land that's so black and rich that it doesn't take any pushing at all to make the flowers and vegetables grow. He has a cow and a beagle and four cats—and about five hundred books. He fixes lawn mowers and boat engines for the people in his area, and he putters away at his funny little house. He writes pieces for the *Digby Courier* and the *Novascotian,* and last winter he confessed to me that he writes poetry. He's childless and wifeless, but he has the time of day for any kid who comes around to hear stories or to have a broken toy fixed. He keeps an old rocker out on the edge of the cliff, where he can sit and watch the tides of Fundy rise and fall. ∾

---

9 **angina:** a heart condition that causes severe chest pain

10 **breakers:** waves that break into foam

11 **stevedore:** a worker who loads and unloads the cargo of ships in a port

12 **Halifax...Digby...Bay of Fundy:** Halifax is a Canadian city and port; Digby is a town at the water's edge in the Western Valley of Nova Scotia; the Bay of Fundy is an inlet between New Brunswick and Nova Scotia

Getting Ready

i'm the thousand-change girl, getting ready for school,
standing in my bedroom ripping pants and shirts from my
body, trying dresses and skirts. father, at the bottom
of the steps is yelling, the bus is coming, here comes
the bus. i'm wriggling into jeans—zippers grinding their
teeth, buttons refusing their holes. my brother, dressed-
in-five-minutes, stands in the hall, t-shirt and bookbag,
saying what's the big problem. i'm kneeling in front of
the closet, foraging for that great-lost-other-shoe.
father, downstairs, offers advice. slacks, he's yelling,
just put on some slacks. i'm in the mirror, matching
earrings, nervous fingers putting the back to the front.
downstairs, the bus is fuming in the yard, farm kids
with cowlicks sitting in rows. everything's in a pile
on the floor. after school, mother will scream, get upstairs
and hang up that mess, but i don't care, i'm the thousand-
change girl, trotting downstairs now looking good, looking
ready for school. father, pulling back from the steps with
disgust, giving me the once over, saying, is that
what you're wearing?

DEBRA MARQUART

RESPONDING TO CLUSTER ONE

HOW DO I FIND OUT WHO I AM?

Thinking Skill DEFINING

1. Describe the character in the cluster with whom you most identified. Review the Concept Vocabulary on page 10 for words to use in your description.

2. In which story in the cluster does a parent have the most influence? Explain.

3. Using a chart such as the one below, rank how well the main character knows herself or himself by the end of the story, using the number 1 for "clueless" and 5 for knowledgeable. Then provide a brief reason for your ranking.

Character	Ranking 1 to 5	Reason for Ranking
The Prince in "Remember Me"	2	*The prince has figured out who he used to be, but he doesn't want to find out who his wife-to-be really is.*
David Raymond in "On Being Seventeen"		
The speaker in "The Changeling"		
The speaker in "Getting Ready"		
Albert in "Be-ers and Doers"		

4. Pick a character from either "Remember Me," "The Changeling," or "Getting Ready," and explain why your character would agree or disagree with the following statement: "The clothes make the person."

Writing Activity: Defining Who You Are

Consider the story "Be-ers and Doers" and decide which best describes you. Now make a list of other words that **define** who you are and that end in "er." For example, you might be a "listener" or "music maker." Then in either prose or poetry, **define** yourself using the words you have chosen.

A Strong Definition

- begins by stating the term to be defined
- lists the various characteristics or qualities of the term
- provides examples
- ends with a final definition

CLUSTER TWO

Where Do I Fit?

Thinking Skill ANALYZING

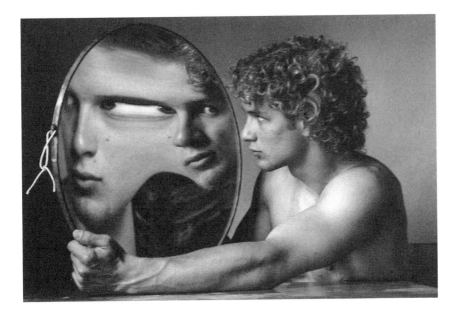

Tiffany, age eleven

Birmingham, Alabama

AS TOLD TO REBECCA CARROLL

What I'd like to say to black girls in America is that it's okay to be who they are and to express what they want to express. And what I'd like to say to white people in America is that I am not offended by their prejudices; if they want to presume that I am offended, then I'm going to presume that it is not my responsibility to educate them in any sort of detail.

My neighborhood is black. I've lived in white neighborhoods, too, and I've been the only black girl in a crowd of white kids. But I've never seen any reason to feel bad about it. There's nothing to feel bad about. In fact, I feel kind of special when I'm the only one. I feel like it's me against the world. I think it's silly to try and look for an experience that has made me feel different or has made me think that my struggle is harder than white people's struggle. You just gotta know who you are, and if you don't know, you can't look anywhere else but inside yourself.

For me, it is very important to have black friends. I have one good, close black friend at school. I also have white friends, but the fact is, if we are talking about something that might be considered "black," like a certain rap group or the language a rap group might use, my white friends are not going to understand, which is fine; they don't have to. Everyone is so upset that black people and white people don't all eat, sleep, and breathe the same everything, but if we did, we'd be in big trouble. I don't feel like I have to explain something like rap music to my white friends. If they want to listen to it, too, that's all right, but I don't

HARLEM GIRL
1925
Winold Reiss

know why they would think that I need to or can explain what it's like to listen to rap music or how I feel about it. And you know they'll ask, too. They'll say, "What is rap music all about?" What am I gonna tell them? Well, it has good beats.

I'm not defensive about the music I listen to and I don't really have a theory about it. But I have seen some videos on television that make me wonder about some of the music I listen to, like Snoop Doggy Dogg.[1] I think he's crazy offensive and I really don't understand why any woman would actually agree to be in his videos knowing that they're going to be exploited like they are. I don't want or need those women to be role models for me, but they do need to think about what they're doing to

1 **Snoop Doggy Dogg:** a rap singer (now known as Snoop Dogg) who
is controversial because of the violence and sexism of his lyrics
and his brushes with the law

themselves and the message they are sending to young people. It's a shame, but if you are black in this society and you have the opportunity to be in front of millions of people, you need to pay attention to what you're doing and how you're doing it, especially if you are a female. It's bad enough that everything on the news talks about black females always being pregnant and on welfare. What's the difference between that and the black females actin' a fool in Snoop Doggy Dogg's videos?

The school I'm at now is good. I went to a much bigger and more diverse school before starting at this one. It hasn't been the easiest transition, but I'm doing all right. I know it's a good opportunity for me. I like my classes and have some good teachers. I like science best, partly because I have a good teacher who takes the time to explain something if I don't understand and partly because I love that science is all about discovery. We do fun and exciting things in class, like go on scavenger hunts where we have to find and identify certain kinds of plants and stuff. I haven't decided what I want to be when I grow up. It's too early, I think, but I know I want to do something that involves discovering ideas and inventing things.

There are no black teachers at my school. The only black adults are the custodians. And that does have an impact on the students, I think. It would be nice to have even one black teacher at the school so that students, both black and white, could see that black people can be teachers, too and not just custodians. And also I think it would be important for the black students to be taught from the perspective of a black adult, not necessarily because there is a "black" way of teaching, but I know that it would be nice to feel like a teacher is talking to me and in some way understanding how I feel about certain things.

I'm not as concerned with black history as I am with black present. I think about black history sometimes, but I feel like it's more important to have the present be good for us. I don't have to think about black history to feel proud. I am *proud* today. I have a really solid family, which I feel lucky about. My mom is the kind of woman who cares a lot about people but doesn't ever go so far as to lose sight of herself. My dad and I are really close. He's a fireman. I haven't gone with him to any fires yet, but I think I will one day. I worry about him sometimes, but then I'll sit down and have a talk with him and feel better. We can talk about anything. He's always there for me. I think his most admirable quality is that he's weird. You know, he's not afraid to do anything at all—I mean anything. He is really fearless.

I have one older brother and he goes to a larger, more diverse school than the school I go to. I think being black means something different for boys than it does for girls. I think for boys everything rides on being tough and being cool. And being cool doesn't include hanging out with white people at all, as in the thought doesn't even fit into the picture. Somehow it seems like black girls can be more comfortable around white people. I don't know why, although I'm sure there's a reason. I just know that there are real serious pressures for black boys in society today and I try not to mess with it too much.

I have close white girlfriends at school. They're close, but not *real* close. There is a fine line between close and real close, but I guess what it really comes down to is trust. And see, it's the same with the way I feel about being black: I don't think about it; I just *know*. With my white friends, I don't think about being close or real close, I just know that there is a difference between being close and real close. For example, I take karate, and I am the only black girl in the class. See, I don't feel like an outcast because I'm pretty good at karate. But then again, one time I was at a karate tournament and I scored the highest on my team as well as against the other team. But the first-place trophy was given to another girl on my team who was white. I was mad, but it's almost like I know things like this are going to happen and it takes a lot of courage to keep getting up and moving on. When you just know things, there isn't a whole lot of time or really much use in trying to figure out why they are what they are.

I claim the right to be Tiffany and Tiffany is many things. I claim the right to play basketball, study science, do karate, listen to rap music, love my parents, be as loud as I please, and have an attitude that separates me from everyone else. My attitude can be all that or real chill, but whatever it is, it's mine. And if anyone has a problem with that, they can speak to me directly. ∾

The Green Killer

M.E. KERR

Be nice to him," my father said. "He's your cousin, after all."

"He takes my things."

"Don't be silly, Alan. What of yours could Blaze possibly want? He has everything . . . *everything,*" my father added with a slight tone of disdain, for we all knew how spoiled my cousin was.

But he did take my things. Not things he wanted because he needed them, but little things like a seashell I'd saved and polished, an Indian head nickel I'd found, a lucky stone shaped like a star. Every time he came from New York City with his family for a visit, some little thing of mine was missing after they left.

We were expecting them for Thanksgiving that year. It was our turn to do the holiday dinner with all our relatives. Everyone would be crowded into our dining room with extra card tables brought up from the cellar, and all sorts of things borrowed from the next-door neighbors: folding chairs, extra serving platters, one of those giant coffee pots that could serve twenty . . . on and on.

It was better when it was their turn and everyone trooped into New York for a gala feast in their Fifth Avenue apartment overlooking Central Park. They had a doorman to welcome us, a cook to make the turkey dinner, maids to serve us.

Blaze's father was the CEO of Dunn Industry. My father was the principal of Middle Grove High School on Long Island. About the only thing the two brothers had in common was a son apiece: brilliant, dazzling Blaze Dunn, seventeen; and yours truly, Alan Dunn, sixteen, average.

But that was a Thanksgiving no one in the family would ever get to enjoy or forget. An accident on the Long Island Expressway caused the cherry black Mercedes to overturn, and my cousin Blaze was killed instantly.

I had mixed emotions the day months later when I was invited into New York to take what I wanted of Blaze's things.

Did I want to wear those cashmere[1] sweaters and wool jackets and pants I'd always envied, with their Ralph Lauren and Calvin Klein labels? The shoes—even the shoes fit me, British-made Brooks Brothers Church's. Suits from Paul Stuart. Even the torn jeans and salty denim jackets had a hyperelegant[2] "preppy" tone.

Yes!

Yes, I wanted to have them! It would make up for all the times my stomach had turned over with envy when he walked into a room, and the niggling awareness always there that my cousin flaunted his riches before me with glee. And all the rest—his good looks (Blaze was almost beautiful with his tanned perfect face, long eyelashes, green eyes, shiny black hair); and of course he was a straight-A student. He was at ease in any social situation. More than at ease. He was an entertainer, a teller of stories, a boy who could make you listen and laugh. Golden. He was a golden boy. My own mother admitted it. Special, unique, a winner—all of those things I'd heard said about Blaze. Even the name, never mind it was his mother's maiden name. Blaze Dunn. I used to imagine one day I'd see it up on the marquee of some Broadway theater, or on a book cover, or at the bottom of a painting in the Museum of Modern Art. He'd wanted to be an actor, a writer, a painter. His only problem, he had always said, was deciding which talent to stress.

While I packed up my garment bags full of his clothes, I pictured him leering down from that up above where we imagine the dead watching us. I thought of him smirking at the sight of me there in his room, imagined him saying, "It's the only way *you'd* ever luck out like this, Snail!" He used to call me that. Snail. It was because I'd take naps when he was visiting. I couldn't help it. I'd get exhausted by him. I'd curl up in my room and hope he'd be gone when I'd wake up . . . He said snails slept a lot, too. He'd won a prize once for an essay he'd written about snails.

---

1 **cashmere:** a fine, soft wool
2 **hyperelegant:** of extremely high quality

He'd described how snails left a sticky discharge under them as they moved, and he claimed that because of it a snail could crawl along the edge of a razor without cutting itself . . . He'd have the whole dining table enthralled while he repeated things like that from his prize-winning essays. And while I retreated to my room to sleep—that was when he took my things.

All right. He took my things; I took *his* things.

I thought I might feel weird wearing his clothes, and even my mother wondered if I'd be comfortable in them. It was my father who thundered, "Ridiculous! Take advantage of your advantages! It's an inheritance, of sorts. You don't turn down *money* that's left you!"

Not only did I not feel all that weird in Blaze's clothes, I began to take on a new confidence. I think I even walked with a new, sure step. I know I became more outgoing, you might even say more popular. Not dazzling, no, not able to hold a room spellbound while I tossed out some information about the habits of insects, but in my own little high-school world out on Long Island I wasn't the old average Alan Dunn plodding along snaillike anymore. That spring I got elected to the prom committee, which decides the theme for the big end-of-the-year dance, and I even found the courage to ask Courtney Sweet out.

The only magic denied me by my inheritance seemed to be whatever it would take to propel me from being an average student with grades slipping down too often into Cs and Ds, up into Blaze's A and A-plus status. My newfound confidence had swept me into a social whirl that was affecting my studies. I was almost flunking science.

When I finally unpacked a few boxes of books and trivia that Blaze's mother had set aside for me, I found my seashell, my Indian head nickel, and my lucky stone . . . And other things: a thin gold girl's bracelet, a silver key ring from Tiffany,[3] initials H. J. K. A school ring of some sort with a ruby stone. A medal with two golf clubs crossed on its face. A lot of little things like that . . . and then a small red leather notebook the size of a playing card.

In very tiny writing inside, Blaze had listed initials, dates, and objects this way:

3 **Tiffany:** an exclusive store in New York City

A.D.	December 25	Shell
H.K.	March 5	Key ring
A.D.	November 28	Indian nickel

He had filled several pages.

Obviously, I had not been the only one whose things Blaze had swiped. It was nothing personal.

As I flipped the pages, I saw more tiny writing in the back of the note-book.

A sentence saying: *"Everything is sweetened by risk."*

Another: *"Old burglars never die, they just steal away.* (Ha! Ha!)*"*

And: *"I dare, you don't. I have, you won't."*

Even today I wonder why I never told anyone about this. It was not because I wanted to protect Blaze or to leave the glorified memories of him undisturbed. I suppose it comes down to what I found at the bottom of one of the boxes.

The snail essay was there, and there was a paper written entirely in French. There was a composition describing a summer he had spent on the Cape, probably one of those "What I Did Last Summer" assignments unimaginative teachers give at the beginning of fall term . . . I did not bother to read beyond the opening sentences, which were "The Cape has always bored me to death, for everyone goes there to have fun, clones with their golf clubs, tennis rackets, and volleyballs! There are no surprises on the Cape, no mysteries, no danger."

None of it interested me until I found "The Green Killer." It was an essay with an A-plus marked on it, and handwriting saying, "As usual, Blaze, you excel!"

The title made it sound like a Stephen King fantasy, but the essay was a description of an ordinary praying mantis[4] . . . a neat and gory picture of the sharp spikes on his long legs that shot out, dug into an insect, and snap went his head!

"You think it is praying," Blaze had written, *"but it is waiting to kill!"*

My heart began pounding as I read, not because of any bloodthirsty instinct in me, but because an essay for science was due, and here was my chance to excel!

---

4 **praying mantis:** a large insect that clasps its prey in forelimbs held up as if in prayer

Blaze had gone to a private school in New York that demanded students handwrite their essays, so I carefully copied the essay into my computer, making a little bargain with Blaze's ghost as I printed it out: *I will not tell on you in return for borrowing your handiwork. Fair is fair. Your golden reputation will stay untarnished, while my sad showing in science will be enhanced through you.*

"The Green Killer" was an enormous hit! Mr. Van Fleet, our teacher, read it aloud, while I sat there beaming in Blaze's torn Polo jeans and light blue cashmere sweater. Nothing of mine had ever been read in class before. I had never received an A.

After class, Mr. Van Fleet informed me that he was entering the essay in a statewide science contest, and he congratulated me, adding, "You've changed, Alan. I don't mean just this essay—but *you*. Your personality. We've all noticed it." Then he gave me a friendly punch, and grinned slyly. "Maybe Courtney Sweet has inspired you."

And she was waiting for me by my locker, looking all over my face as she smiled at me, purring her congratulations.

Ah, Blaze, I thought, *finally, my dear cousin, you're my boy . . . and your secret is safe with me. That's our deal.*

Shortly after my essay was sent off to the science competition, Mr. Van Fleet asked me to stay after class again.

"Everyone," he said, "was impressed with 'The Green Killer,' Alan. Everyone agreed it was remarkable."

"Thank you," I said, unbuttoning my Ralph Lauren blazer, breathing a sigh of pleasure, rocking back and forth in my Church's loafers.

"And why not?" Mr. Van Fleet continued. "It was copied word for word from an essay written by Isaac Asimov.[5] One of the judges spotted it immediately."

So Blaze was Blaze—even dead he'd managed to take something from me once again. ❧

---

5 **Issac Asimov:** author and scientist. Asimov was professor of biochemistry at Boston University, but is better known for his science fiction and fantasy short stories

Plains Indians doll adorned with human hair wig, 1900-10.

The Cutting of My Long Hair

ZITKALA-ŠA

Zitkala-Ša, a Dakota Sioux of the Yankton reservation, was born in 1876. At the age of eight, she traveled with other children of her tribe to White's Manual Institute in Wabash, Indiana. The purpose of this Quaker missionary school was to convert Indians to Christian beliefs and to teach them the ways of white society. In the process, the Indians were required to give up tribal beliefs, cultures, customs, and languages. It was three years before she would return home and see her mother again. In this passage she records her first experiences in a bewildering alien environment.

The first day in the land of apples was a bitter-cold one; for the snow still covered the ground, and trees were bare. A large bell rang for breakfast, its loud metallic voice crashing through the belfry[1] overhead and into our sensitive ears. The annoying clatter of shoes on bare floors gave us no peace. The constant clash of harsh noises, with an undercurrent of many voices murmuring an unknown tongue, made a bedlam[2] within which I was securely tied. And though my spirit tore itself in struggling for its lost freedom, all was useless.

A paleface[3] woman, with white hair, came up after us. We were placed in a line of girls who were marching into the dining room. These were

---

1 **belfry:** a bell tower
2 **bedlam:** a state of uproar and confusion
3 **paleface:** a white person

Indian girls, in stiff shoes and closely clinging dresses. The small girls wore sleeved aprons and shingled[4] hair. As I walked noiselessly in my soft moccasins, I felt like sinking to the floor, for my blanket had been stripped from my shoulders. I looked hard at the Indian girls, who seemed not to care that they were even more immodestly dressed than I, in their tightly fitting clothes. While we marched in, the boys entered at an opposite door. I watched for the three young braves who came in our party. I spied them in the rear ranks, looking as uncomfortable as I felt.

A small bell was tapped, and each of the pupils drew a chair from under the table. Supposing this act meant they were to be seated, I pulled out mine and at once slipped into it from one side. But when I turned my head, I saw that I was the only one seated, and all the rest at our table remained standing. Just as I began to rise, looking shyly around to see how chairs were to be used, a second bell was sounded. All were seated at last, and I had to crawl back into my chair again. I heard a man's voice at one end of the hall, and I looked around to see him. But all the others hung their heads over their plates. As I glanced at the long chain of tables, I caught the eyes of a paleface woman upon me. Immediately I dropped my eyes, wondering why I was so keenly watched by the strange woman. The man ceased his mutterings, and then a third bell was tapped. Every one picked up his knife and fork and began eating. I began crying instead, for by this time I was afraid to venture anything more.

But this eating by formula was not the hardest trial in that first day. Late in the morning, my friend Judéwin gave me a terrible warning. Judéwin knew a few words of English, and she had overheard the paleface woman talk about cutting our long, heavy hair. Our mothers had taught us that only unskilled warriors who were captured had their hair shingled by the enemy. Among our people, short hair was worn by mourners, and shingled hair by cowards!

We discussed our fate some moments, and when Judéwin said, "We have to submit, because they are strong," I rebelled.

"No, I will not submit! I will struggle first!" I answered.

I watched my chance, and when no one noticed I disappeared. I crept up the stairs as quietly as I could in my squeaking shoes,—my moccasins had been exchanged for shoes. Along the hall I passed, without knowing whither[5] I was going. Turning aside to an open door, I found a large room

---

4 **shingled:** cut in the shape of a shingle

5 **whither:** where

with three white beds in it. The windows were covered with dark green curtains, which made the room very dim. Thankful that no one was there, I directed my steps toward the corner farthest from the door. On my hands and knees I crawled under the bed, and cuddled myself in the dark corner.

From my hiding place I peered out, shuddering with fear whenever I heard footsteps near by. Though in the hall loud voices were calling my name, and I knew that even Judéwin was searching for me, I did not open my mouth to answer. Then the steps were quickened and the voices became excited. The sounds came nearer and nearer. Women and girls entered the room. I held my breath and watched them open closet doors and peep behind large trunks. Some one threw up the curtains, and the room was filled with sudden light. What caused them to stoop and look under the bed I do not know. I remember being dragged out, though I resisted by kicking and scratching wildly. In spite of myself, I was carried downstairs and tied fast in a chair.

I cried aloud, shaking my head all the while until I felt the cold blades of the scissors against my neck, and heard them gnaw off one of my thick braids. Then I lost my spirit. Since the day I was taken from my mother I had suffered extreme indignities.[6] People had stared at me. I had been tossed about in the air like a wooden puppet. And now my long hair was shingled like a coward's! In my anguish I moaned for my mother, but no one came to comfort me. Not a soul reasoned quietly with me, as my own mother used to do; for now I was only one of many little animals driven by a herder. ∾

---

6 **indignities:** humiliating treatment

The Way Up

WILLIAM HOFFMAN

Sitting in the back row of English literature class, Jamie looked through an open window toward a rounded silver water tower which poked up through the woods like a great metal tulip. The tower had recently been painted and appeared immaculate in the spring sunlight. Tubular steel legs were hidden at the bottom by newly greening oaks, sycamores, and poplars that bordered the rear grounds of the suburban Richmond High School.

Jamie had made no brag. He had not even spoken the evening he was at Jawbone's house, loafing in the basement playroom with the others.

"Look at Jamie's," Jawbone said. Jawbone was a dark, wiry boy of eighteen who had a jutting chin. He wanted to go to West Point. He stuck a finger on Jamie's picture in the new yearbook. Under the names of the others were accomplishments—teams, organizations, trophies.

"Not even the Glee Club," Nick said, lying on a sofa, his legs hanging over the arm rest at one end. He was a blond boy whose father owned a fancy restaurant downtown.

"They'll never know you been here," Alf said. Alf, the top student, was a heavyset, shaggy boy who'd won his letter in baseball.

More sensitive than the rest, he was immediately sorry. He reached across a chair to punch Jamie's arm. Jamie dodged and smiled, though smiling was like cracking rock.

They meant the remarks good-naturedly. Still, the words made him see what his relationship to them was. He had gone through four years of high school without leaving a mark. He had ridden with them daily, shared their secrets, and eaten in their homes. They considered him a friend. But they expected nothing from him.

At first he was resentful and hurt, as if betrayed. Next he had fantasies of heroic derring-do[1] on the basketball court or baseball diamond—because of his smallness he didn't dream of football glory any longer. After the fantasies, he tried to think of projects. Finally he came up with a plan.

He had spent a lot of time working out details. He was now merely waiting for the right day—or rather night. Recently there had been rain and blustering weather. Even when the sun shone, the wind gusted. This afternoon, however, as he sat in English literature class, Jamie saw that the treetops barely quivered.

His eyes kept returning to the silver water tower. Other students had attempted the climb. A few inventive ones had gone up as far as the catwalk around the fat belly of the tank, where they had painted skulls and crossbones. A sophomore had lost his nerve halfway and got stuck. The Richmond rescue squad had coaxed him down like a kitten from a light pole. The boy had been so ashamed he had tried to join the Army. Nobody had ever made it to the stubby spike on the crown.

Mr. Tharpe, the principal, understood the tower's temptation and had ordered the ladder above the catwalk taken off. He had also directed that the ladder up the leg be cut high above the ground. Lastly, he had made climbing the tower punishable by expulsion.

The toughest problem was getting from the catwalk to the crown. As the tank served only the school, it wasn't large, but without a ladder the rounded sides appeared unscalable. Jamie concluded that he needed a light hook which could be thrown fifteen to twenty feet.

He found what he wanted in a Richmond boating store—a small, three-pronged, aluminum anchor. Along with the anchor he bought fifty feet of braided nylon line that had a thousand-pound test strength. He also purchased a hacksaw. The clerk packed the things in a strong cardboard box, and as soon as Jamie reached home, he hid them in the back of his closet.

He assembled other equipment as well—tennis shoes, a pair of light cotton gloves, a sweat suit, which would keep him warm in the night air yet allow him to move freely, a billed cap, a small flashlight with a holding ring, and a sheath knife to fasten to his leather belt.

Twice he scheduled attempts on the tower. The first night a thunderstorm washed him out. The second, the moon was too bright, increasing the risk that he would be seen.

---

1 **derring-do:** deeds

Delay made him uneasy. He felt that if he didn't go soon, he might lose his nerve.

The bell rang. He went to his locker and then left the building quickly. He wanted to get away without the others seeing him, but Alf called his name. Alf ran down the sidewalk. He adjusted his glasses.

"Want to shoot baskets?" he asked, making an imaginary hook shot. He held up two fingers to indicate a score.

"No, thanks," Jamie answered, moving on.

"You're getting pretty exclusive lately," Alf said.

"I've always been exclusive," Jamie told him, hoping it sounded like a joke.

He spent the afternoon working around the house. He cut the grass and spread some of the lawn fertilizer his father had stored in the garage. When he had a chance, he went up to his room and again checked his equipment. The check was just nervousness. He knew his equipment was right.

After dinner, as he was sure they would, his parents went next door to play cards. He and his brother David were left in the house. David was a year younger, although already heavier than Jamie. He had been asked to come out for football and liked to flex his muscles before a mirror.

Jamie sat at his desk and pretended to study so he wouldn't be questioned. He listened to sounds of the night coming through the open window. There was some wind, but not enough to worry him. The sky was cloudy.

When David went down to the kitchen for a sandwich, Jamie undressed, put on the sweat suit, and pulled pajamas over it. He kept his socks on. He slipped his belt through slots in the leather sheath of the knife and buckled it around his waist. Hearing David approach, Jamie got into bed.

"You sick?" David asked, surprised.

"Just sleepy."

"You look kind of queasy."

"I'm okay."

David watched TV and did his exercises before coming to bed. Jamie listened, as he had for weeks, to the pattern of his brother's breathing. In practice, Jamie had gotten up several times and moved around the dark room. Once David had waked. Jamie had explained he was after another blanket.

David breathed softly. When he was completely asleep, his mouth opened and he wheezed slightly. Jamie heard the wheezing grow. Still he did not move, although he wanted badly to start. He lay on his back, eyes open, waiting for his parents.

They returned at eleven. He heard them in the kitchen. Finally his mother came to his and David's room. Jamie smelled her perfume. She bent over them, lightly adjusting the covers. He kept his eyes shut until she went out.

As soon as she was gone, he swung his legs out of bed. He stood, listening, but David's breathing did not change. Jamie walked to the closet, slipped off his pajamas, and sat on the floor to pull on his tennis shoes. He tied the laces in double knots.

He put on his baseball cap and fastened the large, red bandanna around his neck. The bandanna, too, was part of his plan. He had bought it in a Richmond ten-cent store. For some time he had been carrying it to school and whipping it out to be seen by Jawbone, Nick, and Alf. Though no name was on it, people would identify it as his—the right people, anyway.

Lastly he worked his fingers into the cotton gloves, gathered the hacksaw and aluminum anchor, and tiptoed to the window. It was already half-raised. Earlier in the week he'd rubbed soap along the metal tracks to prevent squeaking.

The window slid up noiselessly. He unsnapped the screen and lifted it out. David turned in his bed but did not wake. Jamie climbed onto the window ledge, lowered his equipment to the ground, and stepped down to the grass of the back yard. He stood still and listened. David did not stir. Jamie replaced the screen without hooking it and picked up his equipment.

Crouching, he ran—not fast enough to wear himself out, but with the easy lope of a distance runner. He carried the anchor in his right hand, the saw in his left. The damp grass of neighboring yards brushed his feet softly. He stayed in the shadows.

On reaching the high school, he cut behind the main building and headed toward the athletic field. When he was almost to the other side, a dog snarled close behind him. He was afraid that if he continued running, the dog might jump him. He turned and ducked behind a pile of canvas tackling dummies.[2]

2 **tackling dummies:** stuffed figures that are used to help football players perfect their techniques for tackling or blocking

The dog leaped out of the dark, its hair bristling, its teeth bared. Jamie talked softly, holding his hands at his sides so as not to excite the boxer. The animal circled, sniffed, and growled.

"King!" a voice from the field house called. It was Carver, the watchman—an erect, dark figure outlined against a door. "Here, boy!"

The dog sprang off toward the field house. Jamie pressed against the ground. Carver leaned over to pat the boxer.

"What's out there?" he asked, turning on his long flashlight. The light brushed across the dummies. Jamie held his breath. Carver talked to the dog. Finally the flashlight went out, and Carver entered the field house. The door slammed.

Jamie pushed up and sprinted. He wanted to be well away in case the boxer was still loose. His arms pumped. By the time he reached the woods, he was winded. There was no use even starting up the tower unless he was fresh. He rested against a tree.

When his breath steadied, he walked on through the woods. He didn't need his flashlight. Clouds had slid away from a sickle[3] moon, which laid a pale sheen on his path. He stopped once to be certain nobody was following.

He walked out of the woods to the tower and under it. Though the tank wasn't large, it was high and seemed to float like a balloon. The silver skin shone eerily. The steel legs were like those of a giant insect poised over him. He touched the steel and kicked a cement footing to rid himself of the sensation. The tank was simply a water tower which could be climbed.

▲ ▲ ▲

He didn't hurry. Hurrying might tire him. Methodically he unwound the line from the anchor. He looped the saw onto his belt. He adjusted his cap. Standing away from a leg of the tower, he swung the anchor around his head like a lasso and let fly at the ladder.

The hooks missed by inches. The light anchor clanged against tubular steel, which reverberated like a gong. The sound was loud—loud enough, perhaps, to alert the watchman or the family who lived in a board-and-batten[4] house nearby. Quickly Jamie picked up the anchor, swung it, and threw. A prong clattered over a rung.

3 **sickle:** crescent-shaped
4 **board-and-batten:** siding in which spaces between siding boards are covered by narrow strips of wood

He had practiced rope climbing. Two or three afternoons a week he had pulled himself to the I-beam at the top of the gym where ropes were attached to swivels. He had learned to go up without using his legs. Basketball players had stood around to watch, impressed that anybody so slight could climb so well.

"You're turning into a regular Atlas," Nick had said.

Jamie had already tied knots every five feet along the nylon line in order to have a better grip on it. He fingered the line and pulled. As he looked up, he felt doubt. The line was thin, the tower great. He jumped before he had time to think further.

Climbing made him feel better. He reached the bottom of the ladder and easily drew himself onto it. He stopped to loosen the anchor. He wrapped the line around the anchor's shank[5] and hooked it over his left shoulder.

He stepped up slowly. He was attempting to pace himself for the distance. He looked neither up nor down. Doing so might cause dizziness. He narrowed his eyes and tried to see no more than his own gloved hands closing over rungs.

After what seemed a long while, he glanced up to get his bearings on the catwalk. He was disappointed at how far it was above him. He estimated that he had come only a quarter of the way. His excitement was giving him a false sense of time.

He kept on. When he again looked up, he had climbed not quite halfway. His breathing was noisy, and he rested. As he clung to the ladder, he thought how easy it would be to go back now. Nobody knew he was here. He could go down and slip into his bed without ever being missed.

He was angry at himself for considering it. His trouble was thinking too much. To block the thoughts, he stepped up, determined to reach the catwalk without stopping again.

He climbed until his arms and legs ached. He sucked at air. He did not raise his eyes lest the distance to the catwalk discourage him. Occasionally a light wind gusted against his face and chest—not hard enough to worry him, but sufficient to slow his step.

His head banged steel. The blow frightened and pained him, and he clutched at the ladder. The catwalk door was right over him, its heavy padlock swinging from his having hit it.

5 **shank:** the straight and narrow part of a tool

He put his right leg through the ladder and hooked the foot over a rung to keep from falling in case he lost his balance. He unbuckled his belt to get the hacksaw. Because of the awkwardness of his position, he had to work slowly. His left hand held the lock, his right the saw.

Cutting was more difficult than he'd anticipated. He had to rest and wipe sweat from his face. When the metal finally snapped, he flung the saw from him. It was a long time hitting the ground.

He threw the padlock down, too, glad he had on gloves in case an investigation checked fingerprints. He raised a hand to the trap door and pushed. The thick iron squeaked but gave only a little. He stepped up another rung in order to hunch his shoulders and the back of his head against it. The door rose, teetered, and fell to the catwalk with a loud clang.

He climbed the rest of the way up the ladder, swung off it to the catwalk, and, holding the railing, closed the trap door. As he straightened to look out over the dark land, he had his first real sense of how high he was. Instinctively, he pressed against the tank. He edged around the catwalk until he faced the school. Lights from houses were faint and twinkling, and he saw the skyline milkiness of Richmond itself.

He grinned, thinking of Alf, Nick, and Jawbone. They wouldn't believe it! They were lying down there, warm in their bunks. He waved a hand over them.

He turned to the tank. He was still a good fifteen feet from the top. As he calculated the distance, a cloud passing over gave him a feeling that the tower was falling. Space shifted under him. He grabbed at the tank.

Leaning against it, he considered tying his bandanna to the railing on the school side. In the morning everybody would see it. Going up this far was certainly a victory, and people would be impressed.

He took off the bandanna and hesitated, fingering it. For tying the bandanna to the railing he might be temporarily honored, but if he was the first to reach the top, he would be remembered for years.

▲　▲　▲

He retied the bandanna around his neck and unwound the nylon line from the anchor. In order to throw to the top of the tank from the proper angle, he had to lean out and flap his arm upward. He forced his thigh hard against the railing. Holding the anchor from him, he threw.

The anchor thumped on top of the rounded tower but slid back when he pulled the line. He jumped to keep from being hit. He stumbled and almost fell. Fear surged in him.

He rested against the tank. When he was calmer, he again threw the anchor. He made half a dozen tries, but each time it came sliding back. He didn't have quite the angle he needed to get the anchor to the crown where the spike was. There was simply no way to do it. He had to tie the bandanna to the railing and climb down.

Another idea nagged him. He shook his head as if he'd been asked. He didn't want to step up onto the railing. He'd be crazy to do it. He could, of course, use part of his line to tie himself. Thus if he slipped, he wouldn't fall far.

He wrapped the nylon line twice around his waist. He knotted the middle section to one of the upright supports of the railing.

Cautiously, like a performer mounting the high wire, he stepped up onto the pipe railing. He rested a hand against the tank so that any fall would be toward the catwalk. His left foot dangled. Though his body wished to bend, he straightened it. He was sweating, and the anchor was wet in his grip. He blinked to clear his eyes, being careful not to turn his head toward where he might look down.

He hefted the anchor and with a gentle, looping motion arched it over himself. The anchor slid back and struck him in the side of the face. Standing on the railing, he was unable to dodge. His head throbbed and ached. He touched his cheek, and his hand came away bloody.

He pulled the anchor up from the catwalk. This time he didn't throw it directly over him. When he tugged on the line, the anchor came down. He felt weak and sick.

He balanced the anchor, tossed it, and jerked the line. The anchor did not come back. He jumped to the catwalk and pulled. The anchor held.

He couldn't be certain it was caught on the spike. Perhaps a hook tip was in a seam or had snagged a bolt. He hung all his weight on the line, drawing up his feet to do so. Next he untied the line from the railing support. He dried his hands on his sweat suit and wiped his mouth.

With a great effort, he pulled himself up. When he reached the rounded curve of the roof, he worked his hands under the line that his weight stretched tight. Nausea pumped through him as he bruised his knuckles on the steel. Grunting, he made a final thrust of his body and lay flat against the slope.

His heart beat hard. He sweated yet felt cold in the gusting wind. He raised his head to look at the top of the tower. Two prongs of the anchor had caught the spike.

He crawled up. Because of the slope and his tennis shoes, he could have done it without a line. He lay on his side as he took off the bandanna. He tied the bandanna high on the spike. He tested to make certain the bandanna would not blow loose.

To go down, he merely let his body slide against the steel. He braked himself by gripping the line. His feet jarred against the catwalk. He hated leaving his anchor, but he knew of no way to pull it free. With his knife, he cut the line as high as he could reach. He wound what was left of it around his body and opened the trap door.

As he put a foot on the ladder, a gust of wind caught his cap and blew it off. He snatched for the cap but missed. It fluttered dizzily down and down and down. He couldn't stop looking. The cap seemed to fall forever. He felt the pull of space. He'd tumble the same way if he slipped. He began to shake. He was too weak to climb down that great distance. He backed off.

Fear ballooned in him, and he shook harder. He couldn't stop thinking of the boy who'd gotten stalled halfway up and needed the Richmond rescue squad. The terrible disgrace of it—the sirens, the people gathered around, and the spotlight swinging up. The police would call his parents.

Yet he was unable to force himself to the ladder. The grip was gone from his fingers, and his body was limp. He might climb down a few steps and not be able to hold. He had the sensation of falling, like the cap, of cartwheeling end over end to the ground. He lay flat on the catwalk, his face against steel strips. He was shaking so badly that his temple knocked against the metal.

He gave himself up to fear. As if his mouth had a life of its own, yells came out. He couldn't stop the sounds. He shouted for help. He screamed and begged in a rush of terror.

The wind carried his voice away. Even if he was missed at home and searched for, nobody would think of looking on the tower. He'd have to lie on the catwalk all night. . . . No, he couldn't! With his flashlight he signaled toward the school. There was no response from the watchman. Jamie kept yelling until his voice became faint and hoarse. He wept.

The fright in him was gradually replaced by exhaustion. He lay panting. He felt the heat of shame. He thought of Alf, Nick, and Jawbone seeing him like this. He thought of his parents. Like a person gone blind, he groped for the trap door.

This time he didn't allow himself to look down. Instead he rolled his eyes upward. His fingers measured the position of the hole, and he lowered a trembling foot to a rung. As if decrepit, he shifted his weight onto the ladder.

He went down a step. He was holding the rungs too tightly, and his sweating hands made the steel slippery. He felt the pull of space behind him. His breathing was rapid and shallow. He moved the way a small child would, using the same foot first on each rung.

He closed his eyes. His body functioned with no direction from him. He was a passenger cowering inside.

He rested, hanging his armpits over the ladder and leaning his forehead against the steel. For an instant he was drunkenly comfortable. He wobbled on the ladder, almost letting go. He caught himself and cried out.

Again he started down. In the endlessness of his descent, he didn't believe he would ever get to the bottom. His hands would fail, and he would drop off. He imagined his body curving to the ground.

He stopped on the ladder, not understanding. The fact that his foot swung under him and found no support meant nothing. He believed his tiredness had tricked him. A second time he put out the foot. Like one coming from a cave into sunlight, he opened his eyes and squinted. He saw the dark shapes of trees. He was at the base of the ladder. Lying under the tower was his cap.

Wearily, even calmly now, he untied the line from his waist and knotted it to the bottom rung. He wrapped the line around his wrists. He slid down, but he was too weak to brake himself effectively. The line burned his skin. When he hit the ground, he fell backward. He lay looking at the silver tower shining above him.

Using one of the tubular steel legs for support, he pulled himself up, staggered, and stooped for his cap. He turned to get his bearings before stumbling into a jogging run. At the trees he wove to a stop and again looked at the tower. He shuddered.

He breathed deeply. Straightening, he entered the dark woods with the step of a man who wouldn't be hurried and walked back toward the house. ∾

Saying Yes

DIANA CHANG

"Are you Chinese?"
"Yes."

"American?"
"Yes."

"*Really* Chinese?"
"No . . . not quite."

"*Really* American?"
"Well, actually, you see . . ."

But I would rather say
yes

Not neither-nor,
not maybe,
but both, and not only

The homes I've had,
the ways I am

I'd rather say it
twice,
yes

RESPONDING TO CLUSTER TWO

WHERE DO I FIT?

Thinking Skill ANALYZING

1. Tiffany makes a number of strong statements in the first selection. Choose one of her statements and explain why you agree or disagree.

2. Rank how much each of the following characters cares about fitting in and **analyze** why. Finally, rank yourself. Use a scale from 1 to 5 with 1 as "not caring at all" and 5 as "caring a great deal."

Character	Ranking	Reason for Ranking
Tiffany	1 2 3 4 5	
Alan	1 2 3 4 5	
Zitkala-Sa	1 2 3 4 5	
Jamie	1 2 3 4 5	
Myself	1 2 3 4 5	

3. Using the **dialog** format of "Saying Yes" as your guide, write a poem about fitting in. The subject of the poem may either be you or a character from one of the stories.

4. What is Jamie trying to achieve by climbing the tower in the story "The Way Up"? In your opinion, does he achieve it?

5. Take the chart on self-knowledge that you started in Cluster 1 and rank the self-knowledge of the characters in this cluster.

Writing Activity: Analyzing the Importance of Fitting In

In most of the selections in this cluster, the main characters weigh the pros and cons of fitting in. **Analyze** the changes these characters make or refuse to make. (To **analyze** means to break something down into parts and study each part). Write a short essay entitled "Fitting In Means. . ." Use examples from your experience or from the selections to support your essay. The chart in question 2 may help you with your analysis.

A Strong Analysis

• states the purpose of the analysis

• demonstrates careful examination of each part of the topic

• supports each point with evidence

• ends with a summary of the ideas presented

CLUSTER THREE

What Do I Believe?

Thinking Skill   EVALUATING

Born Worker

GARY SOTO

They said that José was born with a ring of dirt around his neck, with grime under his fingernails, and skin calloused from the grainy twist of a shovel. They said his palms were already rough by the time he was three, and soon after he learned his primary colors, his squint was the squint of an aged laborer. They said he was a born worker. By seven he was drinking coffee slowly, his mouth pursed the way his mother sipped. He wore jeans, a shirt with sleeves rolled to his elbows. His eye could measure a length of board, and his knees genuflected[1] over flower beds and leafy gutters.

They said lots of things about José, but almost nothing of his parents. His mother stitched at a machine all day, and his father, with a steady job at the telephone company, climbed splintered, sun-sucked poles, fixed wires and looked around the city at tree level.

"What do you see up there?" José once asked his father.

"Work," he answered. "I see years of work, *mi'jo.*"[2]

José took this as a truth, and though he did well in school, he felt destined to labor. His arms would pump, his legs would bend, his arms would carry a world of earth. He believed in hard work, believed that his strength was as ancient as a rock's.

"Life is hard," his father repeated from the time José could first make out the meaning of words until he was stroking his fingers against the grain of his sandpaper beard.

His mother was an example to José. She would raise her hands, showing her fingers pierced from the sewing machines. She bled on her machine,

---

1 **genuflected:** bent as in prayer
2 *mi'jo:* Spanish for "my son"

bled because there was money to make, a child to raise, and a roof to stay under.

One day when José returned home from junior high, his cousin Arnie was sitting on the lawn sucking on a stalk of grass. José knew that grass didn't come from his lawn. His was cut and pampered, clean.

"José!" Arnie shouted as he took off the earphones of his CD Walkman.

"Hi, Arnie," José said without much enthusiasm. He didn't like his cousin. He thought he was lazy and, worse, spoiled by the trappings of being middle class. His parents had good jobs in offices and showered him with clothes, shoes, CDs, vacations, almost anything he wanted. Arnie's family had never climbed a telephone pole to size up the future.

Arnie rose to his feet, and José saw that his cousin was wearing a new pair of high-tops. He didn't say anything.

"Got an idea," Arnie said cheerfully. "Something that'll make us money."

José looked at his cousin, not a muscle of curiosity twitching in his face.

Still, Arnie explained that since he himself was so clever with words, and his best cousin in the whole world was good at working with his hands, that maybe they might start a company.

"What would you do?" José asked.

"Me?" he said brightly. "Shoot, I'll round up all kinds of jobs for you. You won't have to do anything." He stopped, then started again. "Except—you know—do the work."

"Get out of here," José said.

"Don't be that way," Arnie begged. "Let me tell you how it works."

The boys went inside the house, and while José stripped off his school clothes and put on his jeans and a T-shirt, Arnie told him that they could be rich.

"You ever hear of this guy named Bechtel?" Arnie asked.

José shook his head.

"Man, he started just like us," Arnie said. "He started digging ditches and stuff, and the next thing you knew, he was sitting by his own swimming pool. You want to sit by your own pool, don't you?" Arnie smiled, waiting for José to speak up.

"Never heard of this guy Bechtel," José said after he rolled on two huge socks, worn at the heels. He opened up his chest of drawers and brought out a packet of Kleenex.

Arnie looked at the Kleenex.

"How come you don't use your sleeve?" Arnie joked.

José thought a moment and said, "I'm not like you." He smiled at his retort.

"Listen, I'll find the work, and then we can split it fifty-fifty."

José knew fifty-fifty was a bad deal.

"How about sixty-forty?" Arnie suggested when he could see that José wasn't going for it. "I know a lot of people from my dad's job. They're waiting for us."

José sat on the edge of his bed and started to lace up his boots. He knew that there were agencies that would find you work, agencies that took a portion of your pay. They're cheats, he thought, people who sit in air-conditioned offices while others work.

"You really know a lot of people?" José asked.

"Boatloads," Arnie said. "My dad works with this millionaire—honest—who cooks a steak for his dog every day."

He's a liar, José thought. No matter how he tried, he couldn't picture a dog grubbing on steak. The world was too poor for that kind of silliness.

"Listen, I'll go eighty-twenty," José said.

"Aw, man," Arnie whined. "That ain't fair."

José laughed.

"I mean, half the work is finding the jobs," Arnie explained, his palms up as he begged José to be reasonable.

José knew this was true. He had had to go door-to-door, and he disliked asking for work. He assumed that it should automatically be his since he was a good worker, honest, and always on time.

"Where did you get this idea, anyhow?" José asked.

"I got a business mind," Arnie said proudly.

"Just like that Bechtel guy," José retorted.

"That's right."

José agreed to a seventy-thirty split, with the condition that Arnie had to help out. Arnie hollered, arguing that some people were meant to work and others to come up with brilliant ideas. He was one of the latter. Still, he agreed after José said it was that or nothing.

In the next two weeks, Arnie found an array of jobs. José peeled off shingles from a rickety garage roof, carried rocks down a path to where a pond would go, and spray-painted lawn furniture. And while Arnie accompanied him, most of the time he did nothing. He did help occasionally. He did shake the cans of spray paint and kick aside debris so that José didn't trip while going down the path carrying the rocks. He did stack the piles of shingles, but almost cried when a nail bit his thumb. But mostly he told José what he had missed or where the work could be improved. José was bothered because he and his work had never been criticized before.

But soon José learned to ignore his cousin, ignore his comment about his spray painting, or about the way he lugged rocks, two in each arm. He didn't say anything, either, when they got paid and Arnie rubbed his hands like a fly, muttering, "It's payday."

Then Arnie found a job scrubbing a drained swimming pool. The two boys met early at José's house. Arnie brought his bike. José's own bike had a flat that grinned like a clown's face.

"I'll pedal," José suggested when Arnie said that he didn't have much leg strength.

With Arnie on the handlebars, José tore off, his pedaling so strong that tears of fear formed in Arnie's eyes.

"Slow down!" Arnie cried.

José ignored him and within minutes they were riding the bike up a gravel driveway. Arnie hopped off at first chance.

"You're scary," Arnie said, picking a gnat from his eye.

José chuckled.

When Arnie knocked on the door, an old man still in pajamas appeared in the window. He motioned for the boys to come around to the back.

"Let me do the talking," Arnie suggested to his cousin. "He knows my dad real good. They're like this." He pressed two fingers together.

José didn't bother to say OK. He walked the bike into the backyard, which was lush with plants—roses in their last bloom, geraniums, hydrangeas, pansies with their skirts of bright colors. José could make out the splash of a fountain. Then he heard the hysterical yapping of a poodle. From all his noise, a person might have thought the dog was on fire.

"Hi, Mr. Clemens," Arnie said, extending his hand. "I'm Arnie Sanchez. It's nice to see you again."

José had never seen a kid actually greet someone like this. Mr. Clemens said, hiking up his pajama bottoms, "I only wanted one kid to work."

"Oh," Arnie stuttered. "Actually, my cousin José really does the work and I kind of, you know, supervise."

Mr. Clemens pinched up his wrinkled face. He seemed not to understand. He took out a pea-sized hearing aid, fiddled with its tiny dial, and fit it into his ear, which was surrounded with wiry gray hair.

"I'm only paying for one boy," Mr. Clemens shouted. His poodle click-clicked and stood behind his legs. The dog bared its small crooked teeth.

"That's right," Arnie said, smiling a strained smile. "We know that you're going to compensate only one of us."

Mr. Clemens muttered under his breath. He combed his hair with his fingers. He showed José the pool, which was shaped as round as an elephant. It was filthy with grime. Near the bottom some grayish water shimmered and leaves floated as limp as cornflakes.

"It's got to be real clean," Mr. Clemens said, "or it's not worth it."

"Oh, José's a great worker," Arnie said. He patted his cousin's shoulders and said that he could lift a mule.

Mr. Clemens sized up José and squeezed his shoulders, too.

"How do I know you, anyhow?" Mr. Clemens asked Arnie, who was aiming a smile at the poodle.

"You know my dad," Arnie answered, raising his smile to the old man. "He works at Interstate Insurance. You and he had some business deals."

Mr. Clemens thought for a moment, a hand on his mouth, head shaking. He could have been thinking about the meaning of life, his face was so dark.

"Mexican fella?" he inquired.

"That's him," Arnie said happily

José felt like hitting his cousin for his cheerful attitude. Instead, he walked over and picked up the white plastic bottle of bleach. Next to it were a wire brush, a pumice stone,[3] and some rags. He set down the bottle and, like a surgeon, put on a pair of rubber gloves.

"You know what you're doing, boy?" Mr. Clemens asked.

José nodded as he walked into the pool. If it had been filled with water, his chest would have been wet. The new hair on his chest would have been floating like the legs of a jellyfish.

"Oh yeah," Arnie chimed, speaking for his cousin. "José was born to work."

José would have drowned his cousin if there had been more water. Instead, he poured a bleach solution into a rag and swirled it over an area. He took the wire brush and scrubbed. The black algae came up like a foamy monster.

3 **pumice stone:** a stone made from volcanic material used for smoothing and polishing

"We're a team," Arnie said to Mr. Clemens.

Arnie descended into the pool and took the bleach bottle from José. He held it for José and smiled up at Mr. Clemens, who, hands on hips, watched for a while, the poodle at his side. He cupped his ear, as if to pick up the sounds of José's scrubbing.

"Nice day, huh?" Arnie sang.

"What?" Mr. Clemens said.

"Nice day," Arnie repeated, this time louder. "So which ear can't you hear in?" Grinning, Arnie wiggled his ear to make sure that Mr. Clemens knew what he was asking.

Mr. Clemens ignored Arnie. He watched José, whose arms worked back and forth like he was sawing logs.

"We're not only a team," Arnie shouted, "but we're also cousins."

Mr. Clemens shook his head at Arnie. When he left, the poodle leading the way, Arnie immediately climbed out of the pool and sat on the edge, legs dangling.

"It's going to be blazing," Arnie complained. He shaded his eyes with his hand and looked east, where the sun was rising over a sycamore, its leaves hanging like bats.

José scrubbed. He worked the wire brush over the black and green stains, the grime dripping like tears. He finished a large area. He hopped out of the pool and returned hauling a garden hose with an attached nozzle. He gave the cleaned area a blast. When the spray got too close, his cousin screamed, got up, and, searching for something to do, picked a loquat[4] from a tree.

"What's your favorite fruit?" Arnie asked.

José ignored him.

Arnie stuffed a bunch of loquats into his mouth, then cursed himself for splattering juice on his new high-tops. He returned to the pool, his cheeks fat with the seeds, and once again sat at the edge. He started to tell José how he had first learned to swim. "We were on vacation in Mazatlán.[5] You been there, ain't you?"

José shook his head. He dabbed the bleach solution onto the sides of the pool with a rag and scrubbed a new area.

"Anyhow, my dad was on the beach and saw this drowned dead guy," Arnie continued. "And right there, my dad got scared and realized I couldn't swim."

4 **loquat:** a small yellow fruit that grows on a type of evergreen tree

5 **Mazatlán:** a port city on the Pacific coast of Mexico

Arnie rattled on about how his father had taught him in the hotel pool and later showed him where the drowned man's body had been.

"Be quiet," José said.

"What?"

"I can't concentrate," José said, stepping back to look at the cleaned area.

Arnie shut his mouth but opened it to lick loquat juice from his fingers. He kicked his legs against the swimming pool, bored. He looked around the backyard and spotted a lounge chair. He got up, dusting off the back of his pants, and threw himself into the cushions. He raised and lowered the back of the lounge. Sighing, he snuggled in. He stayed quiet for three minutes, during which time José scrubbed. His arms hurt but he kept working with long strokes. José knew that in an hour the sun would drench the pool with light. He hurried to get the job done.

Arnie then asked, "You ever peel before?"

José looked at his cousin. His nose burned from the bleach. He scrunched up his face.

"You know, like when you get sunburned."

"I'm too dark to peel," José said, his words echoing because he had advanced to the deep end. "Why don't you be quiet and let me work?"

Arnie babbled on that he had peeled when on vacation in Hawaii. He explained that he was really more French than Mexican, and that's why his skin was sensitive. He said that when he lived in France, people thought that he could be Portuguese or maybe Armenian, never Mexican.

José felt like soaking his rag with bleach and pressing it over Arnie's mouth to make him be quiet.

Then Mr. Clemens appeared. He was dressed in white pants and a flowery shirt. His thin hair was combed so that his scalp, as pink as a crab, showed.

"I'm just taking a little rest," Arnie said.

Arnie leaped back into the pool. He took the bleach bottle and held it. He smiled at Mr. Clemens, who came to inspect their progress.

"José's doing a good job," Arnie said, then whistled a song.

Mr. Clemens peered into the pool, hands on knees, admiring the progress.

"Pretty good, huh?" Arnie asked.

Mr. Clemens nodded. Then his hearing aid fell out, and José turned in time to see it roll like a bottle cap toward the bottom of the pool. It leaped into the stagnant water with a plop. A single bubble went up, and it was gone.

"Dang," Mr. Clemens swore. He took shuffling steps toward the deep end. He steadied his gaze on where the hearing aid had sunk. He leaned over and suddenly, arms waving, one leg kicking out, he tumbled into the pool. He landed standing up, then his legs buckled, and he crumbled, his head striking against the bottom. He rolled once, and half of his body settled in the water.

"Did you see that!" Arnie shouted, big-eyed.

José had already dropped his brushes on the side of the pool and hurried to the old man, who moaned, eyes closed, his false teeth jutting from his mouth. A ribbon of blood immediately began to flow from his scalp.

"We better get out of here!" Arnie suggested. "They're going to blame us!"

José knelt on both knees at the old man's side. He took the man's teeth from his mouth and placed them in his shirt pocket. The old man groaned and opened his eyes, which were shiny wet. He appeared startled, like a newborn.

"Sir, you'll be all right," José cooed, then snapped at his cousin. "Arnie, get over here and help me!"

"I'm going home," Arnie whined.

"You punk!" José yelled. "Go inside and call 911."

Arnie said that they should leave him there.

"Why should we get involved?" he cried as he started for his bike. "It's his own fault."

José laid the man's head down and with giant steps leaped out of the pool, shoving his cousin as he passed. He went into the kitchen and punched in 911 on a telephone. He explained to the operator what had happened. When asked the address, José dropped the phone and went onto the front porch to look for it.

"It's 940 East Brown," José breathed. He hung up and looked wildly about the kitchen. He opened up the refrigerator and brought out a plastic tray of ice, which he twisted so that a few of the cubes popped out and slid across the floor. He wrapped some cubes in a dish towel. When he raced outside, Arnie was gone, the yapping poodle was doing laps around the edge of the pool, and Mr. Clemens was trying to stand up.

"No, sir," José said as he jumped into the pool, his own knees almost buckling. "Please, sit down."

Mr. Clemens staggered and collapsed. José caught him before he hit his head again. The towel of ice cubes dropped from his hands. With his legs spread to absorb the weight, José raised the man up in his arms, this fragile man. He picked him up and carefully stepped toward the shallow end, one slow elephant step at a time.

"You'll be all right," José said, more to himself than to Mr. Clemens, who moaned and struggled to be let free.

The sirens wailed in the distance. The poodle yapped, which started a dog barking in the neighbor's yard.

"You'll be OK," José repeated, and in the shallow end of the pool, he edged up the steps. He lay the old man in the lounge chair and raced back inside for more ice and another towel. He returned outside and placed the bundle of cubes on the man's head, where the blood flowed. Mr. Clemens was awake, looking about. When the old man felt his mouth, José reached into his shirt pocket and pulled out his false teeth. He fit the teeth into Mr. Clemens's mouth and a smile appeared, something bright at a difficult time.

"I hit my head," Mr. Clemens said after smacking his teeth so that the fit was right.

José looked up and his gaze floated to a telephone pole, one his father might have climbed. If he had been there, his father would have seen that José was more than just a good worker. He would have seen a good man. He held the towel to the old man's head. The poodle, now quiet, joined them on the lounge chair.

A fire truck pulled into the driveway and soon they were surrounded by firemen, one of whom brought out a first-aid kit. A fireman led José away and asked what had happened. He was starting to explain when his cousin reappeared, yapping like a poodle.

"I was scrubbing the pool," Arnie shouted, "and I said, 'Mr. Clemens, you shouldn't stand so close to the edge.' But did he listen? No, he leaned over and . . . Well, you can just imagine my horror."

José walked away from Arnie's jabbering. He walked away, and realized that there were people like his cousin, the liar, and people like himself, someone he was getting to know. He walked away and in the midmorning heat boosted himself up a telephone pole. He climbed up and saw for himself what his father saw—miles and miles of trees and houses, and a future lost in the layers of yellowish haze. ᴑ

Dolly's False Legacy

IAN WILMUT

The announcement in February 1997 of the birth of a sheep named Dolly, an exact genetic replica of its mother, sparked a worldwide debate over the moral and medical implications of cloning. Several U.S. states and European countries have banned the cloning of human beings, yet South Korean scientists claimed recently that they had already taken the first step. In the following essay for Time, *embryologist[1] Wilmut, who led the team that brought Dolly to life at Scotland's Roslin Institute, explains why he believes the debate over cloning people has largely missed the point.*

Overlooked in the arguments about the morality of artificially repro-
ducing life is the fact that, at present, cloning is a very inefficient procedure. The incidence of death among fetuses and offspring produced by cloning is much higher than it is through natural reproduction—roughly 10 times as high after birth in our studies at Roslin. Distressing enough for those working with animals, these failure rates surely render unthinkable the notion of applying such treatment to humans.

Even if the technique were perfected, however, we must ask ourselves what practical value whole-being cloning might have. What exactly would be the difference between a "cloned" baby and a child born natu-rally—and why would we want one?

1 **embryologist:** a biologist that studies the development of embryos
in mammals

The cloned child would be a genetically identical twin of the original, and thus physically very similar—far more similar than a natural parent and child. Human personality, however, emerges from both the effects of the genes we inherit (nature) and environmental factors (nurture).[2] The two clones would develop distinct personalities, just as twins develop unique identities. And because the copy would often be born in a different family, cloned twins would be less alike in personality than natural identical twins.

Why "copy" people in the first place? Couples unable to have children might choose to have a copy of one of them rather than accept the intrusion of genes from a donor. My wife and I have two children of our own and an adopted child, but I find it helpful to consider what might have happened in my own marriage if a copy of me had been made to overcome infertility.[3] My wife and I met in high school. How would she react to a physical copy of the young man she fell in love with? How would any of us find living with ourselves? Surely the older clone—I, in this case—would believe that he understood how the copy should behave and so be even more likely than the average father to impose expectations upon his child. Above all, how would a teenager cope with looking at me, a balding, aging man, and seeing the physical future ahead of him?

Each of us can imagine hypothetical[4] families created by the introduction of a cloned child—a copy of one partner in a homosexual relationship or of a single parent, for example. What is missing in all this is consideration of what's in the interests of the cloned child. Because there is no form of infertility that could be overcome only by cloning, I do not find these proposals acceptable. My concerns are not on religious grounds or on the basis of a perceived intrinsic[5] ethical principle. Rather, my judgment is that it would be difficult for families created in this way to provide an appropriate environment for the child.

Cloning is also suggested as a means of bringing back a relative, usually a child, killed tragically. Any parent can understand that wish, but it must first be recognized that the copy would be a new baby and not the lost child. Herein lies the difficulty, for the grieving parents are seeking not a new baby but a return of the dead one. Since the original would be

2 **nurture:** training or upbringing

3 **infertility:** inability to have children

4 **hypothetical:** made up for the sake of discussion

5 **intrinsic:** inborn or basic

fondly remembered as having particular talents and interests, would not the parent expect the copy to be the same? It is possible, however, that the copy would develop quite differently. Is it fair to the new child to place it in a family with such unnatural expectations?

What if the lost child was very young? The shorter the life, the fewer the expectations parents might place on the substitute, right? If a baby dies within a few days of birth and there is no reason to think that death was caused by an inherited defect, would it then be acceptable to make a copy? Is it practical to frame legislation that would prevent copying of adults or older children, but allow copying of infants? At what age would a child be too old to be copied in the event of death?

Copying is also suggested as a measure by which parents can have the child of their dreams. Couples might choose to have a copy of a film star, baseball player or scientist, depending on their interests. But because personality is only partly the result of genetic inheritance conflict would be sure to arise if the cloned child failed to develop the same interests as the original. What if the copy of Einstein shows no interest in science? Or the football player turns to acting? Success also depends upon fortune. What of the child who does not live up to the hopes and dreams of the parents simply because of bad luck?

Every child should be wanted for itself, as an individual. In making a copy of oneself or some famous person, a parent is deliberately specifying the way he or she wishes that child to develop. In recent years, particularly in the U.S., much importance has been placed on the right of individuals to reproduce in ways that they wish. I suggest that there is a greater need to consider the interests of the child and to reject these proposed uses of cloning.

Moreover, there is a lot we do not know about the effects of cloning, especially in terms of aging. As we grow older, changes occur in our cells that reduce the number of times they can reproduce. This clock of age is reset by normal reproduction during the production of sperm and eggs; that is why children of each new generation have a full life span. It is not yet known whether aging is reversed during cloning or if the clone's natural life is shortened by the years its parent has already lived. Then there is the problem of the genetic errors that accumulate in our cells. There are systems to seek out and correct such errors during normal reproduction; it is not known if that can occur during cloning. Research with animals is urgently required to measure the life span and determine the cause of death of animals produced by cloning.

Important questions also remain on the most appropriate means of controlling the development and use of these techniques. It is taken for granted that the production and sale of drugs will be regulated by governments, but this was not always the case. A hundred years ago, the production and sale of drugs in the U.S. was unregulated. Unscrupulous[6] companies took the opportunity to include in their products substances, like cocaine, that were likely to make the patients feel better even if they offered no treatment for the original condition. After public protest, championed by publications such as the *Ladies' Home Journal,* a federal act was passed in 1906. An enforcement agency, known now as the FDA, was established in 1927. An independent body similar to the FDA is now required to assess all the research on cloning.

There is much still to be learned about the biology associated with cloning. The time required for this research, however, will also provide an opportunity for each society to decide how it wishes the technique to be used. At some point in the future, cloning will have much to contribute to human medicine, but we must use it cautiously. ❧

---

6 **unscrupulous:** not ethical

Moon

CHAIM POTOK

Moon Vinten, recently turned thirteen, was short for his age and too bony, too thin. He had a small pale face, dark angry eyes, and straight jet-black hair. A tiny silver ring hung from the lobe of his right ear, and a ponytail sprouted below the thick band at the nape of his neck and ran between his angular shoulder blades. The ponytail, emerging like a waterfall from the flat-combed dark hair, was dyed the clear blue color of a morning sky.

Moon marched into the family den one autumn evening and announced to his parents that he wanted to build a recording studio for himself and his band.

His parents, short, slender people in their late forties, had been talking quietly on the sofa. Moon's father, annoyed by his son's brusque interruption of the conversation, thought: First, those drums; then the earring and the ponytail. And now a *recording studio?* In a restrained tone, he asked, "What, exactly, does that involve?"

"A big table, microphones, stands, extension cords, rugs or carpets for soundproofing, a mixing board,"[1] said Moon.

"And how will you pay for all that?"

"With the money I got for my birthday."

Patience is the desired mode here, Moon's father told himself. "I'll remind you again. That money has been put away for your college tuition."

"The band will make lots of money, Dad."

---

1 **mixing board:** instrument that controls microphone levels and equalizes the bass or treble in amplified music

"Then buy the equipment with that money."

"We'll need money to buy the equipment so we can make really high-quality recordings," said Moon, trying to keep himself calm. "We'll demo the recordings and send them out, and start making money from the gigs we'll get. It takes money to make money, Dad."

Moon's father turned to Moon's mother. "Where is he learning these things, Julia?"

"He's your son, too, Kenneth," said Moon's mother. "Why don't you ask him?" Her mind at that moment was on another matter: the face of a boy in Pakistan.

"He's only thirteen years old, for God's sake," Moon's father said.

Moon hated it when they talked about him as if he weren't there. His parents, who were physicians, spoke often to each other clinically[2] about their patients, and at times about Moon as if he were a patient. It was one more irritant in the list of things that made him angry.

2 **clinically:** coolly and unemotionally

"We shouldn't attach an 'only' to a thirteen-year-old," said his mother, still seeing the face of the Pakistani boy, whose photograph had come to her office in the morning mail. "A thirteen-year-old is not a child."

Moon's father, a precise man with a dry, intimidating manner, looked at Moon and asked, "Where, exactly, do you plan to put all that equipment?"

"In the garage," Moon replied.

His parents stared at him. Calm is called for, his father thought, and remained silent. Inside Moon's mother, an unassuming woman of gentle demeanor, the picture of the gaunt, brown-faced Pakistani boy—dry thin lips, small straight nose, enormous frightened eyes—abruptly winked out.

She said quietly to Moon, "Dear, we keep our cars in the garage."

Moon said, "Then I'll put it in the basement."

"We've been through all that," said Moon's father—the clamor erupting from the basement and streaming through the air ducts and filling the house with that booming drumming twanging pandemonium they called music. "Let's talk about it another time."

"When, Dad?"

"Soon."

"But when?"

His father said, "Morgan, I have very important calls to make." Morgan was Moon's given name, first on the list of things that made him angry. A jovial older cousin had called him Moon some years ago, for a reason Moon could no longer remember. His parents and his teachers still called him Morgan.

"I need the phone to call the guys in the band," said Moon.

"Whoever is on the phone, if an overseas call comes in on call waiting, please tell me immediately," said Moon's mother.

"I need the phone," said Moon again.

"Don't you have any homework?" his father asked.

"Dad, I really really really need to talk to the guys in my band," said Moon.

Moon's parents sat very quietly on the couch, looking at their son. Even excited or angered, his face retained its pallid look. But his dark eyes glittered, and his thin lips drew back tight over his small white teeth as if keeping a seal on a poisonous boil of words.

The telephone rang.

Moon's father picked up the receiver and said crisply, "Dr. Vinten." He listened and handed the receiver to Moon's mother. "Pakistan," he said.

Moon, his hands clenched, turned and left the den.

▲ ▲ ▲

He took the carpeted stairs two at a time to the second floor, and as he threw open the door to his room, the anger erupted. His heart raced, his hands shook. He felt the rage like a scalding second skin. He slammed the door shut. The large color photograph of the Beatles, tacked loosely to the inside of the door, fluttered briefly; the Beatles seemed to be dancing and undulating in their costumes.

He flopped down on his bed.

Always with the fury came fear. Occasional tantrums had accompanied him through childhood and in recent years had become too-frequent fits of rage that rose suddenly from deep inside him and sometimes took possession of his body. He lay on his back, tight and quivering. "When you feel it coming, stop what you're doing," Mrs. Graham, the school counselor, had advised. "Take deep breaths and count slowly." He counted: One . . . two . . . three . . . Mrs. Graham was a round-faced, good-hearted woman. "If you feel you're losing control, walk out of the classroom. I've told your teachers it's all right for you to do that." Four . . . five . . . six . . . It was after his fight with Tim Wesley two weeks before, when they pummeled each other and tumbled down the wide staircase into the school's main entrance hall. Seven . . . eight . . . nine . . . Later, Moon couldn't remember why the fight had begun. His parents and Mrs. Graham had discussed the possibility of Moon getting help. A therapist, a total stranger. Everything he'd say would be written down, probably recorded. Ten . . . eleven . . .twelve . . . Maybe go up to the third floor and play the drums awhile. But he needed the telephone.

Was that someone at the door?

He got down off the bed and pulled the door open and saw his mother standing in the hallway.

She said gently, "I keep reminding you, if you close your door, we can't communicate with you. Closed doors often turn into stone walls."

His mother's frequent moralizing was definitely on the list of things that made Moon angry. "Can I use the phone now?" he asked.

She sighed. "I came up to tell you that we'll be having a guest."

"Who?" asked Moon.

"A boy from Pakistan."

Children with rare diseases came to his parents from all over the world for diagnosis and treatment. But always to the hospital, never to the house.

He asked, "Why is he staying with us if he's sick?"

His mother said, "He's not sick, dear. An organization your father and I belong to is bringing him into the country. You'll hear about it in school."

"He's coming to my school?"

"Yes. Be nice to him, dear."

But Moon was imagining the boy wandering around the house and coming upon the small room on the third floor. He took a deep breath and said, "Can I use the phone now, Mom?"

Moon's mother remembered when her second son had gone off to college the year before. "It's difficult to let go, but it's much worse to hold on," she had said to Moon's father, and Moon, listening nearby, had suddenly and unaccountably run up to his room and slammed his door shut with such force that, to the disquiet of his father, the paint cracked near the ceiling on the hallway wall. She now gazed sadly at her youngest son, so different from the ambitious older ones: Andrew in engineering and football; Colin in pre-med and crew.[3] And Morgan—so edgy and sullen, so fixed upon himself.

"Yes, dear, you may use the phone," she said. She was still standing in the hallway, looking at Moon, when he closed the door.

He sat at his cluttered desk and dialed the telephone. Pete's father answered. "Peter is doing his homework," he said.

"This won't take long, Mr. Weybridge. I promise," said Moon.

"You just make sure of that," said Pete's father.

While waiting for Pete to come to the phone, Moon sat looking at the large photographs on the wall across from his bed: John Bonham[4] and Stewart Copeland,[5] playing the drums. And at the photographs on the wall near his bed: George and Paul with their guitars; Ringo at his drums; John singing. He imagined himself sauntering over to them and taking the sticks from Ringo and starting with a light *tik tik tik tik* on the Hi-Hat,[6] and then—

"Hey, hey," came Pete's voice over the phone. "How you doin', Moon?"

"We can jam after school tomorrow, Pete."

"That's cool."

"Hey, Pete, there's a kid from Pakistan who's going to be staying in my house."

---

3 **crew:** the sport of racing in boats propelled by oars

4 **John Bonham:** a legendary drummer with the rock group *Led Zeppelin*

5 **Stewart Copeland:** the drummer who formed the *Police*

6 **Hi-Hat:** a pair of cymbals operated by a foot pedal

"He's stayin' with *you?* Hey, that's real cool!"

"You know about him?"

"Everybody knows."

"How come I never heard anything about him?"

"Hey, you're asleep half the time. And the other half, you're so angry you don't know what's happenin'."

"I need to call Ronnie and John about tomorrow."

"Stay cool, Moon," said Pete.

Moon called Ronnie Klein and then John Wood. Just as he was telling John the time of their jam session, he heard the beep of the call waiting and told John to hang up. Another item on the list of things that angered him: the way call waiting broke into his conversations with his only friends, the members of his band. The low beep, once, twice; most of the calls were for his parents. They wouldn't give him his own telephone; they didn't want him talking on it hours on end; his brothers hadn't had their own telephones, and neither would he.

"This is Dr. Moraes," a voice said in a strange accent. "I am phoning from Pakistan for Dr. Julia Vinten."

"Just a minute, please," said Moon, and he opened his door and called downstairs. "Mom, it's for you."

"Thank you, dear." His mother's voice came to him from the den.

When he returned to his desk, he put the receiver to his ear and heard: "Yes, Dr. Vinten, the boy will arrive early tomorrow. He will no doubt be tired, but he is—"

Moon hung up the telephone.

He had not thought to ask his mother where the boy would be sleep. In Andy's room? In Colin's room? He feared the dusky silences in the house that enlarged the absence of his brothers and magnified invisible presences like the noises the squirrels made scampering inside the walls. Moon imagined he heard his brothers' voices: they were teaching him to hold a bat, catch a hardball, throw a football, dribble a basketball; they were teasing him, calling him the skinny runt of the family; they were helping him with his homework; they were bickering with Mom and Dad over cars and girls and late nights out. The thought of the boy from Pakistan staying in the room of one of his brothers. . . .

Feeling an outrage at his very center, Moon began counting. One . . . two . . . three . . . four . . . He inserted a Pearl Jam CD into his player— five . . . six . . . seven—and put on his earphones, then opened one of the textbooks on the desk. He tapped his index and middle fingers on the desk, *doom-d-d-ka-doom-doom-d-ka-doom-d-d-ka-doom-doom-d-ka,* playing as if he were at a drum and snare. The words in the book flickered and pulsated in the torrent of drums and music.

▲   ▲   ▲

Moon sat slumped in the seat, dimly aware of the TV cameras and crews in the back of the crowded auditorium, the empty chairs on the stage, and the whispering among the students and teachers. School assemblies—almost always full of monotonous, preachy fake talk—were high on the list of things that annoyed Moon and made him angry.

He was especially angry that morning. Mrs. Woolsten had raked him for not handing in the weekly English essay. She was a fat, ugly woman, with thick glasses and a voice like ice water. She wanted the essay tomorrow, and absolutely no excuses. He'd sensed the smirks of his classmates and saw out of the corner of his eye Pete's sympathetic look. He hadn't been able to think of anything to write about and, listening to Mrs. Woolsten's public scolding, had felt heat rise to his face. He'd considered walking out of the room, but instead he'd remained at his desk, counting to himself, fingers tapping silently on his knees . . . until the assistant principal's reedy voice came over the public address system, announcing the special assembly.

The crowd in the auditorium had fallen silent. Moon, still slumped in his seat, watched as some people emerged from the dark right wing of the stage and walked toward the chairs. The first was Dr. Whatley, the school principal; then came two men Moon didn't know, both dressed in dark suits; then a tall, brown-skinned man with glasses and wearing a baggy light-brown suit, followed by a brown-skinned boy about Moon's age but an inch or two shorter than Moon. He looked gaunt. His eyes were dark and enormous. He wore dark trousers and a sky-blue woolen sweater, a white shirt and a tie. His neck stuck out from the collar of the shirt like the neck of a plucked bird.

Behind the boy walked Moon's mother and father.

Moon watched as they all sat down in the chairs on the stage. The boy, looking tense and fearful, seemed not to know what to do with his hands. He sat on the edge of his chair, leaning forward and staring apprehensively at the crowded auditorium.

Dr. Whatley approached the podium and began to speak. Moon closed his eyes and wondered how he could convince his parents to let him build a recording studio. Maybe ask them for an addition to the garage. How much would that cost? Dr. Whatley droned on, his words amplified.

Moon felt itchy, impatient. There was a scattering of applause and some more talk.

A moment later, an odd-sounding voice filled the air, small and breathless and high, and Moon opened his eyes and saw the boy standing behind the podium, only his face and neck visible. Alongside the boy stood the brown-skinned man.

Moon vaguely recalled having heard that the boy's name was Ashraf.

The boy said something in a foreign language, and the man, who had been introduced as Mr. Khan, translated.

The boy spoke again. He was talking about someone named Mr. Malik and the dozen boys who worked in his carpet factory. He said the boys had been bought by Mr. Malik from their parents.

Bought? thought Moon. *Bought?*

The boy said that he himself had been bought at the age of five, for twelve dollars. He told of sitting on a bench fifteen hours a day as a carpet weaver with the others in a long, airless room, two weak lightbulbs burning from a ceiling fixture and the temperature often over one hundred degrees and the mud walls hot when he put his hands to them and the single window closed against carpet-eating insects. But that was better than working in a quarry,[7] hauling and loading stones onto carts for the building of roads, or in the sporting goods factory owned by one of the many nephews of Mr. Malik, making soccer balls by hand eighty hours a week in silence and near darkness. At the carpet looms, he'd worked from six in the morning to eight at night, and sometimes around the clock, tying short lengths of thin thread to a lattice[8] of heavy white threads. His fingers often bled, and the blood mixed with the colors of the threads.

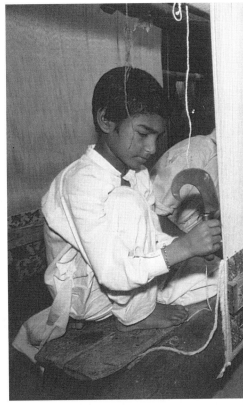

7 **quarry:** an open excavation from which stone and rock are taken

8 **lattice:** a framework or structure of crossed pieces of wood or other materials

"Look," he said, thrusting his hands palms upward across the podium, his thin wrists jutting like chicken bones from the sleeves of his sweater, and Moon—listening to the quavery words of the boy and the deep voice of Mr. Khan—tried to make out the fingers from across the length of the auditorium and could not, and he gazed at his own long, bony fingers and tapped them restlessly on his knees.

The audience was silent.

The boy went on talking in his high, breathless voice. Three weeks ago, in the village where he worked, two men in suits accompanied by two uniformed policemen had entered Mr. Malik's carpet factory and taken him away, along with four younger boys and three older ones. What a shouting Mr. Malik had raised! How dare they take away his workers, his boys? All legally acquired from their parents—he had the papers to prove it, documents signed and recorded with the proper authorities! The boy paused and then said, Was it right that children were made to labor at carpet factories, at brick and textile factories, at tanneries[9] and steelworks? He said, People in America shouldn't buy the carpets made in his country. If the carpet makers couldn't sell their carpets, they wouldn't have any reason to use children as cheap labor.

He stopped, peering uncertainly at Mr. Khan, who nodded and smiled. The boy thanked the audience for listening to him and walked back to his chair and sat down. He put his hands on his knees and gazed at the floor. All the adults on the stage were looking at him.

There was an uneasy stirring in the audience and nervous, scattered applause.

Moon sat very still looking at the boy.

Dr. Whatley stepped to the podium and introduced one of the two strangers, who turned out to be the governor of the state. The second stranger was the head of the organization that had brought the boy to the United States. Moon didn't listen to them. Nor did he pay much attention to the brief talks given by his parents; each said something about the need to raise the consciousness of Americans. He was watching the boy, who sat on the edge of his chair, leaning forward and appearing a little lost—and wasn't it strange how right there on the stage, in front of everyone, as first the governor and then the head of the organization and then Moon's parents spoke, wasn't it strange how Ashraf had begun to tap with his fingers on his knees, lightly and silently tapping in small movements

9 **tanneries:** places where animal hides are made into leather

to some inner music he seemed to be hearing? Moon watched the rhythm and pattern of Ashraf's tapping, an odd sort of tempo, unlike anything Moon had ever seen before, and found himself tapping along with him. A one one one and a two and a one and a two and . . .

In the school lunchroom later that day, Moon was at a table with Pete and the two other members of his band when Ashraf entered with Mr. Khan. He saw them go along the food line and then carry their trays to a table and sit with some other students. Moon watched Ashraf eating and heard him respond to questions put to him by the students and translated by Mr. Khan. Where had he been born? What sort of food did he like? Had he ever heard of McDonald's or Walt Disney or Tom Hanks? Did he like rock and roll?

As the last question was translated, Ashraf's eyes grew wide and bright, and he nodded. What was his favorite band? He said radiantly, smiling for the first time, "The Beatles," pronouncing it "Bee-ah-tles."

"He says," Mr. Khan translated, "that someone near the carpet factory played recordings of the Beatles very often and very loud." Students crowded around the table, blocking Moon's view. Someone asked who was Ashraf's favorite Beatle, and Moon heard the eager, high-voiced answer: "Ringo."

Minutes later, the crowd around Ashraf thinned, and Moon saw him drumming lightly on the table surface with a knife and fork. Next to him sat Mr. Khan, finishing his meal. About a half-dozen students stood near the table, watching Ashraf's drumming.

"Hey, man," Moon heard Pete say. "You talk to your mom and dad about the recording studio?"

"Yeah," said Moon, looking at Ashraf.

"What'd they say?"

"They're thinking about it."

"Man, that'd be so cool," said Pete. "Our own studio and everything."

Moon wished Pete would be quiet so he could see and hear more clearly Ashraf's oddly rhythmed drumming.

▲　▲　▲

"What's up, man?" said Pete into the telephone later that afternoon. "I got one foot out the door."

"We can't jam today, Pete," said Moon.

"What's happenin'?"

"The kid from Pakistan and his interpreter, they're in my house, sleeping. We can't make any noise."

"He must be tired, man."

"I don't like him sleeping in Andy's bed. And the man, he's in Colin's bed."

"Hey, you know what my dad once said to me? He said, 'You have your own house, you can decide who sleeps there.' "

"We'll jam tomorrow."

"Tomorrow I got my guitar lesson. The day after."

"Okay, Pete."

"Stay cool, man."

Moon called the other two members of the band. Then he sat at the desk in his room, listening to the silence in the house. Two hours at the drums—gone. He thought of Ashraf's head on Andy's pillow. Did they carry diseases? Mom would know about that. His parents were at the hospital; and that evening they were to have dinner with Ashraf and Mr. Khan, along with the governor and the mayor. Moon would eat alone at home, as he did on occasion. He would put a CD into the stereo player in the den, fill the air with swelling, pounding music that drove away the ominous silences and muffled the occasional chittering and scurrying of the squirrels inside the walls of the house.

A noise took him from his thoughts: barely audible voices in the next room. Ashraf and Mr. Khan. Moon rose and left his room. He walked past his parents' bedroom to the door at the end of the hallway and climbed the wooden staircase to the third floor.

The sloping roof of the large stone-and-brick house left space for three small rooms beneath the angled beams: a cedar closet; a storage area for his parents' files; and, the third, the room where Moon played his drums and jammed with his band. There was barely enough space for the chairs and the music stands and the table with the CD player and the small cassette recorder they used to tape some of their sessions. The crowded room was the only place in the house where his parents would permit Moon and his band to play.

He removed the covers from his drums, sat down, popped The Police into the CD player, put on the earphones, and took up his sticks. He knew by heart Stewart Copeland's stroke and beat, and he played with deft precision. The blue-dyed ponytail moved from side to side and bobbed on his shoulders and back.

He played for some time, felt himself gliding off into the surge and crash of the drums and lifted into the cascades of thumping rhythms— and then he sensed an alien presence behind him, and he stopped and turned.

Ashraf and Mr. Khan were in the room.

Moon stared at them. He turned off the CD player and removed his earphones.

"We apologize if we are disturbing you," said Mr. Khan very politely.

"It's okay," said Moon, trying to keep the anger out of his voice. This was what he had feared most: an invasion of his most secret place! Slow, deep breaths . . . One . . . two . . .

Mr. Khan said, "Ashraf has asked me to tell you that your walls make sounds. He heard noises that woke him."

"Those are squirrels," said Moon. "Sometimes they get inside our walls. Usually we only hear them at night." Three . . . four . . . five . . .

Mr. Khan spoke to Ashraf, who nodded and responded.

"He says to tell you the walls of the factory where he worked were filled with insects and sometimes he would hear them at night."

Moon said, "We once had a nest of honeybees in one of our walls. My parents had to bring in a man who raised bees to take away the nest with the bees still in it." Why am I telling him this? Six . . . seven . . .

Ashraf listened attentively to the translation, nodding, then spoke softly.

"He says he does not know your name," said Mr. Khan.

"My name is Moon."

Mr. Khan looked puzzled.

"M-o-o-n," said Moon, spelling his name.

"Ah, yes?" said Mr. Khan. "Moon." He spoke to Ashraf, who responded.

"He asks why are you named Moon."

"It's my name, that's all," said Moon.

Mr. Khan spoke to Ashraf, who gazed intently at Moon. Dark, glittering pupils inside enormous, curious, eager eyes.

"Ashraf says he was drawn here by the sound of your drums and asks if he may speak frankly and put certain—um, how to say it?—personal questions to you."

"Personal? What do you mean, personal?"

"He says he will not be hurt if you do not answer."

"What questions?"

"First, he wishes to ask why you wear a ring in your ear."

"Why I wear the earring? I just do, that's all."

"Ashraf says he does not understand your answer."

"It makes me feel different. You know, not like everyone else."

"He asks why you dye your long hair blue."

"I saw it in a magazine."

"He says if you saw it in a magazine and are doing what others do, how does it make you different?"

Moon felt heat rising to his face. "No one else in my school does it."

"He asks if he may touch your hair."

"What?"

"May he touch your hair?"

Moon took a deep breath. All those questions, and now this. Touch my hair. Well, why not? He turned his head to the side. The ponytail swayed back and forth, dangling blue and loose from its roots of raven hair. Ashraf leaned forward, ran his fingers gently through the ponytail, touching and caressing the sky-blue strands, a look of wonder on his thin face. Then he withdrew his hand. Moon saw him examining his fingers and heard him speak softly to Mr. Khan.

"He says he likes the way your hair looks and feels," Mr. Khan said to Moon.

Moon looked at Ashraf, who smiled back at him shyly and spoke again to Mr. Khan.

"Now he asks why you play the drums."

Moon said, after a brief hesitation, "I just like to."

"He says to tell you that he plays drums because it is sometimes a good feeling to hit something."

"Yeah, I feel that way, too . . . sometimes."

Moon had never before talked about these matters with anyone.

"He says to thank you for your answers."

"Can I ask a question?"

"Of course."

"Why did he work in that factory? Why didn't he just run away?"

Mr. Khan translated, and Ashraf lowered his eyes as he responded.

"He says there was nowhere to run. He was hundreds of miles from his home and would have starved to death or been caught and brought back to his master and very severely beaten and perhaps chained to his workbench or sold off to work in the quarries."

"Why did his parents sell him?"

Ashraf listened to the translation and seemed to fill with shame.

"They needed the money to feed themselves and their other children."

"Does he have to go back?"

"Oh, yes. He feels obligated to return. Our organization will send him to school, and he will continue in the struggle to help other boys like him."

"Please say that I wish him good luck."

Mr. Khan translated, and Ashraf replied.

"He thanks you and asks if he may request of you a small favor."

"Sure."

"He asks if he may play your drums."

Moon, surprised, was silent. His drums! No one touched his drums, ever. He looked at Ashraf, who, after a moment, spoke again.

"He says he will not damage them," said Mr. Khan.

"Well, okay," Moon said.

Ashraf's eyes lit up as he extended his fingers toward Moon. Moon handed him his sticks and slid off the chair. Ashraf took the sticks, sat in Moon's chair, and tapped on Moon's drums. He tapped on the drums and the Hi-Hat, a bit awkwardly and with no apparent rhythm, and after a while he put down the sticks and picked up the bongos from the floor near the Hi-Hat. Holding the bongos between his knees, he began to tap out with his callused fingers and palms the odd rhythm he had played in the auditorium and lunchroom, a one one one and a two and a one and a two and . . .

Moon reached over and switched on the tape recorder.

Ashraf drummed on. Moon, standing next to him, felt the power and pull of the strange rhythm. Ashraf played for some while, *dum dat, dum dat, dum dat,* and sweat formed on his brow and beads of sweat flecked off his face as he played and his fingers became a blur, *dum dat, dum dat, dum dat*—and abruptly he stopped. His eyes were like glowing coals. Sweat streamed down his brown face. He placed the bongos on the floor.

Moon switched off the recorder.

There was a silence before Ashraf spoke.

"He thanks you for the opportunity to play your drums," said Mr. Khan.

"Well, sure, it's okay, you're welcome," said Moon.

"He says you and he will probably never see each other again, but he will remember you."

Moon looked at Ashraf, who briefly spoke again.

"He says we must now leave and prepare for this evening's dinner," said Mr. Khan.

Ashraf extended his hand. Moon took it and was startled by its boniness, its coarse, woodlike callus covering. Smiling shyly, Ashraf shook Moon's hand and then turned and left the small room, followed by Mr. Khan.

Moon rewound a portion of the tape, checked to see that it had recorded properly, and took it down to his room.

▲　▲　▲

Pete asked, "Hey, you see him on TV?"

"See who?" replied Moon. They were walking up the crowded stairs to their English class.

"That kid, what's his name, Ashraf."

"Was he on TV?"

"Man, what planet you livin' on? He was on the news last night and on the *Today* show this mornin'."

"I was writing that essay for Mrs. Woolsten."

"Is he still at your house?"

"He left before I woke up," said Moon.

That evening, he sat with his parents in the den, watching a national news report that showed Ashraf speaking at a high school in Baltimore. He looked small and frightened behind the podium, but he thrust out his hands defiantly to show his fingers. Mr. Khan stood beside him, translating.

The next evening, Ashraf was seen on television appearing before a committee of Congress. He wore a dark suit and a tie, and his neck protruded from the shirt collar. He sat at a long table with Mr. Khan. Moon saw Ashraf's fingers tapping silently from time to time on the edge of the table.

One of the congressmen asked a question. Moon saw Ashraf thrust his hands toward the members of the committee, showing his fingers.

"Spunky kid," said Moon's father. "He's going back to a bad situation."

"Nothing will happen to him, Kenneth. Too many eyes are watching," said Moon's mother.

When Moon came down to breakfast the following morning, he found his father at the kitchen table, tense and upset. His mother, almost always too cheerful for Moon in the early hours of the day, looked troubled.

"What's happening?" Moon asked.

"See for yourself," said his father, and, handing Moon the morning newspaper, pointed to the final paragraph of an essay titled "Blunt Reply to Crusading Boy," on the op-ed page.[10]

Moon read the paragraph:

In conclusion, we hold that there is room for improvement in any society. But we feel that the present situation is acceptable the way it is. The National Assembly must not rush through reforms without first evaluating their impact on productivity and sales. Our position is that the government must avoid so-called humanitarian measures that harm our competitive advantages.

The essay was signed by someone named Imram Malik.

Moon asked, "What does it mean, Dad?"

"You're thirteen years old—what do you think it means?"

"I don't know," said Moon, afraid he understood it too well.

"They would not dare harm him," said his mother.

Moon felt a coldness in his heart, and the impotence that was the prologue to rage.

In the weeks that followed he played the recording often, at times taking it upstairs to the third floor and listening to it and remembering the darkly glittering blaze in Ashraf's eyes when he'd played the bongos. And that's where Moon was the winter night the portable telephone rang on the table where he'd set it, near the tape recorder. It was someone from Washington, D.C., calling his mother. His parents weren't home, he said, and wrote down an unfamiliar name and number. He turned off the telephone, and immediately it rang again, and a man's voice asked for his father. Moon was writing down the man's name and number when he heard the beep of the call waiting and felt himself growing angry. What was he, his parents' secretary or something? He'd come upstairs to play the drums, not to take their phone calls one after the other like that.

"Hey, Moon." It was Pete.

"Hey, Pete. What's up?"

"You heard the news, man?"

"What news?"

"It was just on TV. That Ashraf kid. He's dead."

"What?"

10 **op-ed page:** a page of special features, usually opinion pieces, on the page opposite the editorial page of a newspaper

"He's dead, man. Run down on his bike by a truck. Hit and run."
Moon's hands began to shake.

"They're sayin' it was an accident, but no one believes it for a minute," said Pete.

A fury was boiling in Moon's stomach and flaring red in his eyes. Breathe slowly . . .

"I'm tellin' you, man, they should've burned down all those factories," Pete said, loud and angry. "Only language some people understand."

Moon remained quiet. One . . . two . . . three . . . four . . .

"Hey, man," said Pete. "You there?"

"Yeah," said Moon.

"Your parents home?"

"No." Five . . . six . . . seven . . .

"You want me to come over?"

"No."

"You sure you're okay?"

"Yeah." Eight . . . nine . . . ten . . .

"I gotta go. It's late. We'll talk tomorrow."

Moon turned off the telephone and the tape recorder and sat for a while in the silent room. He removed the tape from the recorder, brought it down to his room, and placed it in his desk drawer. Then he sat at his desk and began to tap a rhythm on its surface with his hands. He played rudiments[11] and patterns and flams.[12] Right right left left right right left left . . . right left right right . . . left right left left . . . flamadiddle paradiddle . . .

Was that someone at his door? He got up and opened the door and saw his parents in the hallway. They were in dinner clothes.

Moon and his parents looked at one another a moment.

"I see you know what happened," said his father.

"Pete called me," said Moon.

"It's horrible," his mother said. Her eyes were red, her face was pale.

"Did they really kill him?" asked Moon.

"Our people in Washington are investigating it," said his father.

"We were up on the third floor together," said Moon. "I made a tape recording of him playing my bongos."

"You did?" said his father, looking surprised.

---

11 **rudiments:** any of several basic patterns in drumming

12 **flams:** drumbeats of two strokes; the first is a quick grace note

"I liked him," said Moon.

Moon saw his parents glance at each other.

"Oh, you poor dear," said his mother.

"We had no idea at all those people would do something that extreme," said his father.

Moon's heart pounded and his skin burned. He stepped back into his room, closing the door. The poster of the Beatles flapped briefly.

The telephone rang twice, and stopped. A moment later someone tapped on his door again.

It was his mother. "Dear, I keep reminding you, if you keep your door closed, we can't communicate with you. Your English teacher is on the phone."

Moon left the door open and went over to the desk and lifted the receiver. "Hello," he said.

Moon's English teacher, Mrs. Woolsten, said, "Morgan, the essay you handed in about your meeting with Ashraf is very good. You wrote that you made a tape recording of him playing the bongos. Is that right?"

"Yeah," said Moon.

"Please bring it with you next Monday."

"Bring the recording to school?"

"Will you do that?"

"Sure," Moon heard himself say.

"And will you bring your drums?"

"My drums?"

"There will be a memorial service for Ashraf."

"Well, yeah, sure, I'll bring my drums," Moon said.

He sat for a while at the desk, then went downstairs and asked if he could borrow his father's tape recorder. Back in his room, he duplicated the tape of Ashraf playing the bongos.

The following Monday morning, he and his father loaded the drums into the car. Moon sat in the back while his parents rode in front, his father behind the wheel. It was a cold, windy day, the sky ice blue. They said nothing to one another during the trip to the school.

Pete met them in the parking lot and helped Moon carry his drums into the auditorium and set them up on the stage near the podium.

Later that morning, the entire school filed silently into the auditorium. From the dark right wing of the stage emerged Dr. Whatley, followed by the mayor, Moon's parents, and Moon. They sat down in chairs on the stage. Dr. Whatley stepped up to the podium and said that they had assembled to honor the memory of the brave boy named Ashraf who had spoken in their school some weeks before and been killed in a recent accident in Pakistan. He talked about how some people left behind records of their lives—books and music, works of art, deeds. He said that Ashraf had decided to live a life of deeds on behalf of young people his age. He announced that a special school fund would be set up in his memory.

Moon sat in his chair on the stage, listening.

The mayor spoke; then Moon's parents. Then, at a nod from Dr. Whatley, Moon went over to his drums and sat down.

A moment passed, and then over the public address system came the sound of the bongos being played by Ashraf.

Moon waited a minute or two and then began to play an accompaniment to the bongos inside the spaces of Ashraf's beat, a one e and a two e and a three e. His Hi-Hat played the ands, and the snare did two and four, and he added ghost notes to the snare, to make it dance, and then added the bell and slipped into the Seattle sound, *doom-do`ak-doom-d`doom-ak,* and the bongos went *dum dat, dum dat, dum dat,* in that strange rhythm, and then Moon took the drums higher in volume and then was taking them higher still, his sticks beating a frenzied cadence, a rhythm of scalding outrage, and he was thumping, driving, throbbing, tearing through his instruments, pouring onto the world a solid waterfall of sound, and he felt the outrage in his arms and shoulders and heart and the sublime sensation of secret power deep in the very darkest part of his innermost soul.

The bongos fell silent. With a crashing flurry, Moon climaxed the drumming, washed in sweat, strands of his blue-dyed hair clinging to his face and neck. He sat with his head bowed, breathing hard and feeling an exhilaration that he knew would be too quickly gone.

A void followed, a gap in time, and utter silence from the audience. Moon, slowly raising his head, saw his parents staring at him, their faces like suddenly illumined globes. Over the public address system came the hollow hissing sound that signaled the end of the recording of Ashraf playing the bongos. ∾

I'm Nobody

EMILY DICKINSON

I'm Nobody! Who are you?
Are you—Nobody—Too?
Then there's a pair of us?
Don't tell! they'd advertise—you know!

How dreary—to be—Somebody!
How public—like a Frog—
To tell one's name—the livelong June—
To an admiring Bog!

RESPONDING TO CLUSTER THREE

WHAT DO I BELIEVE?

Thinking Skill EVALUATING

1. Dolly's False Legacy" examines the issue of human cloning. List three pros and cons of cloning to help **evaluate** what you believe about this issue.

2. Does the speaker in "I'm Nobody" have self-confidence? Explain.

3. Use the chart below to **evaluate** whether the characters in this cluster see themselves as "somebodies" or "nobodies," and whether you think they are "somebodies" or "nobodies." Be prepared to explain your responses.

Character	How Character Sees Self Somebody or Nobody?	How You See Character Somebody or Nobody?
José in "Born Worker		
Arnie in "Born Worker"		
Ashraf in "Moon"		

4. If you had to choose a subtitle for Moon that would express the story's main idea, or **theme**, would it be: "Moon: A Boy Learns to Control His Anger"; "Moon: Music Is a Universal Language"; or "Moon: Tragedy Forces Boy to Care About Others"? Explain your choice or write your own subtitle and tell why you think it expresses the main idea of the story.

5. Sometimes it takes a test or crisis to find out what you believe. What crises face Jose in "Born Worker" and Moon in "Moon"? Explain in a short paragraph what these tests teach the characters about what they believe.

6. Take the chart on self-knowledge that you started in Cluster 1 and rank the self-knowledge of the characters in this cluster.

Writing Activity: Creating a Credo

Evaluate what you believe and then write a credo, or statement of belief, entitled "Suitable for Framing."

To Create a Credo

- brainstorm a list of your beliefs in four categories: family, school, community, and one category of your own choosing, such as friends, recreation, or religion
- narrow your list to three core beliefs
- find a compelling but simple way to state each belief
- combine the statements into a pleasing whole

CLUSTER FOUR

Thinking On Your Own

Thinking Skill   SYNTHESIZING

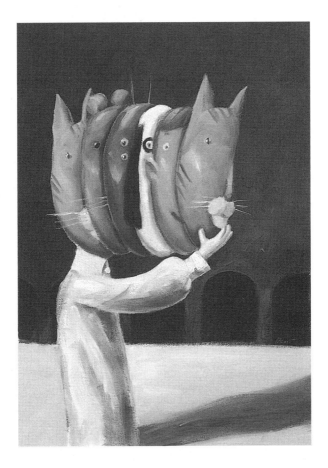

Fairy Tale

TODD STRASSER

Cynthia Durella's stepmother, Ruth, was a witch. She may have lived in a large and fancy apartment on Park Avenue, but it didn't help her disposition one bit. She still had a lot of unresolved anger toward her first husband and it manifested itself in two ways: compulsive shopping and meanness toward her stepdaughter.

"Cynthia darling," Ruth would say after dinner, thoughtfully lifting a bright red fingernail to her bright red lips. "Would you be a dear and do the dishes and take out the garbage and straighten up the kitchen?"

Ruth seemed to believe that as long as she called Cynthia "darling" and "dear" she could make her do all the housework she wanted.

Cynthia always complied. This stepfamily deal was new to her and she didn't want to make trouble, especially since her father was in Europe and the Far East most of the time doing something with petrodollars.[1]

But after weeks of doing the dishes and cleaning the kitchen every night, Cynthia finally asked, "Why can't Sheri do it once in a while?"

Sheri was Ruth's daughter, the same age as Cynthia. But that's where the similarity ended. While Cynthia was slim and had an Ivory Soap complexion, Sheri weighed 156 pounds and had monster zits.

Ruth's mascaraed eyes narrowed into slits. "Sheri has a condition."

"Yeah, dish soap gives me hives," Sheri whined—her normal tone of voice.

Cynthia had never heard of a condition that prevented someone from doing the dishes, but she wasn't surprised. Sheri was a raving hypochondriac[2] and Ruth pampered her to the extreme.

---

1 **petrodollars:** money made in the oil industry
2 **hypochondriac:** a person who often imagines sickness

In the kitchen Cynthia pulled on yellow Playtex gloves. It wasn't so bad, really. Ruth ordered out every night, so there were no pots, just glasses and plates to be rinsed and put in the dishwasher. And leftovers to be saved in the refrigerator for Sheri's multiple late-night snacks. Cynthia's own mother, who'd died in a car accident five years earlier, used to order out a lot too. But that was because she worked full time. Ruth didn't work. She just shopped.

Cynthia was sweeping the kitchen floor when Sheri came in for her first snack. It wasn't even half an hour since dinner, and at dinner she'd inhaled two egg rolls, an order of steamed dumplings, an order of sweet-and-sour pork, a whole big bag of Chinese noodles and a Dove Bar for dessert. Sheri opened the refrigerator and rooted around for a while before coming up with half a family-sized bag of peanut M & M's.

"The fall cotillion is in two weeks," she said, popping five M & M's into her mouth at once.

"What's that?" Cynthia asked.

"It's this dance they hold at school every fall. Everyone gets dressed up. This year it's masquerade."

"Sounds good," Cynthia said.

"Too bad you can't go," Sheri said as she munched on another handful of M & M's. Zit fertilizer.

"Huh? Why not?"

"Well, Mom and your father are going away for the weekend and someone has to walk Honey Plum at exactly eleven o'clock or you know what happens."

Honey Plum was Ruth's neurotic poodle who had to be walked four times a day like clockwork or he'd head for the most expensive Persian rug in the house and do it there out of spite. Cynthia assumed it had something to do with being male and named Honey Plum.

"How come *I* have to walk him?" Cynthia asked.

"Because I can't," Sheri said, downing another handful of candy. "He pulls so hard on the leash that I could dislocate my shoulder. I'm prone to that, you know."

Cynthia rolled her eyes. "I could go and just leave early, couldn't I?"

"Oh, sure," Sheri said. "Except no one shows up till ten and the school doesn't let dances go past twelve thirty. So if you left to walk Honey Plum you'd miss the best part."

Nothing seemed to delight Sheri more than giving bad news. She would have made a great weather forecaster.

"Can't we find someone else to walk Honey Plum?" Cynthia asked.

"No way," Sheri said. "You know he only lets members of the family walk him."

How could Cynthia forget? She'd walked Honey Plum at least twice a day since she'd moved in.

"Besides," Sheri said snidely, "what would you wear? You've got to go in something really fabulous, not the rags you've got in your closet."

"You went through my closet?" Cynthia was shocked.

"Oh, please." Sheri sighed. "Enough with the Little Miss Innocence routine, okay?" She took the bag of M & M's and went into her air-conditioned bedroom to watch television and grow fatter. Cynthia finished sweeping the floor, but she was in no rush to go to her room, which was tiny and right next to the kitchen and had no air conditioning or TV. Ruth, in fact, called it "the maid's room."

Instead she went out to the living room and sat on the white flower-print couch next to the window. Under the couch Honey Plum growled. Except for when nature called, he rarely came out. Cynthia couldn't blame him. Twelve stories below, cars raced up and down Park Avenue, their lights beginning to glow in the darkening evening. Cynthia picked up a fluffy couch pillow and hugged it. She missed the little suburban town she'd grown up in. People were nicer there, softer and more cognizant of each other's feelings. And they didn't go through your closets.

▲   ▲   ▲

Cynthia found it difficult to make new friends at the exclusive Roper School. Everyone had their cliques, and all they talked about were their summer vacations in Europe, their preschool shopping sprees at Bergdorf's,[3] and their weekends dancing all night at L'Image and Tunnel.[4] Even Sheri was in a clique of overweight girls who went around saying cleverly snide things about people and pretending they were Dorothy Parker.[5]

One day Cynthia was eating lunch alone in the dining room (at Roper the word *cafeteria* was frowned on) when she heard a voice behind her say, "You've got to be strong, hon. They're like sharks here. At the first sign of weakness they'll eat you alive."

---

3 **Bergdorf's:** a high quality department store

4 **L'Image and Tunnel:** nightclubs

5 **Dorothy Parker:** American writer of the 30s and 40s, known for her sarcastic humor

Startled, Cynthia turned around and found a tall boy standing behind her. His skin was as pale as Greta Garbo's,[6] his long scraggly reddish hair obscured most of his face, and he wore several earrings and black eyeliner. His clothes were baggy and all black.

"Were you talking to me?" Cynthia asked.

"Who else, hon?" he said, placing his tray next to hers. "Do you mind the French style of dining? I think it's much more civilized than staring at each other with food dripping off our chins."

Cynthia shook her head in amazement as the boy placed his tray next to hers and sat down with a great flourish of arms and legs. His tray contained a single cup of lemon yogurt.

"I was born Stephen Alexander Morganson, but you can call me Sam," he said. "And don't bother telling me your story, hon. It's always the same. You're the victim of divorce and remarriage, cast into these opulent premises by absentee parents who can't remember why they had children in the first place."

Cynthia giggled. "And what's your story?"

Sam smiled and something sparkled in his front tooth. "I am the illegitimate son of Calvin Klein."

Cynthia soon learned that straight answers were not something Sam specialized in. Just who his parents were and how he came to the Roper School remained a mystery, but he was friendly and clever and never failed to make her laugh. Within a week they'd become good friends.

"The key to a successful year at Roper is the cotillion," Sam said one day after school as they window-shopped along Madison Avenue. "The current cliques are all holdovers from last year. Everyone's waiting for the cotillion to see who this year's stars will be."

"Stars?" Cynthia said, skeptically.

"Oh, absolutely, hon. The cotillion sets the tone for the whole year. I mean, if you come back from a Caribbean Christmas vacation with a truly spectacular tan, or a story about meeting someone from the royal family, you might move up a few notches, but otherwise the cotillion etches your fate in stone."

"How?"

"It's all in who asks you to dance, hon."

They stopped outside Ungaro's, the French fashion store. The mannequins were draped in fabulous off-the-shoulder black evening dresses.

---

6 **Greta Garbo:** a beautiful movie star of the 30s who had a fair complexion

Cynthia pictured herself wearing one to the cotillion, but it was a silly fantasy. She couldn't afford a dress like that and she had to walk Honey Plum anyway.

"Something wrong, hon?" Sam asked.

"It's so depressing," Cynthia said with a shrug. "Everything in New York is so competitive. It's like distilled down to the rawest animal instincts. But instead of survival of the fittest, it's survival of the richest and most beautiful."

"So what else is new?" Sam smirked.

"Suppose I don't want to compete?" Cynthia asked. "Suppose I don't even want to go to the cotillion because I think it's silly and superficial? Does that automatically mean I'll be an outcast?"

Sam smiled. "No, hon. It only means you're chicken."

▲ ▲ ▲

Sheri stayed out of school for two days while she and Ruth shopped around town for the perfect cotillion costume gown. At Roper, Cynthia wandered glumly through her classes, trying to convince herself that it didn't matter.

One afternoon she sat with Sam in the library while he critiqued each person who entered through the sculpted wooden doors.

"Now, that's what you call a unibrow," Sam whispered about a girl whose dark eyebrows joined above the bridge of her nose. "Retro-caveperson chic."

Cynthia smiled weakly.

"Why the mope, hon?" Sam asked.

"Oh, I don't know," she replied. "I guess I hate myself for being afraid to go to the dance, but at the same time I hate myself for even caring about it in the first place."

"Ah." Sam raised a finger. "The classic approach-avoidance conflict."

"What should I do?" Cynthia asked.

Before Sam could answer, the doors to the library swung open again and a tall young man came in. He had broad shoulders and dark hair and blue eyes. Everyone in the library seemed to stop what they were doing to stare at him, Cynthia included.

"Conner Worthington Harkness the Third," Sam whispered. "Captain of the lacrosse team. Heir to the Harkness water bed fortune. Around school they call him The One."

"The One?"

"The one every girl wants."

"He must have a girlfriend," Cynthia said.

"He was seeing Rebecca Beaumaster last year, but she went to Greece over the summer and hasn't come back."

"Will he be at the cotillion?"

Sam's eyebrow went up. "Do I sense that approach is suddenly outweighing avoidance?"

▲   ▲   ▲

That night Sheri tried on her costume, which she and Ruth had picked up at Bendel's for a small fortune, along with shoes and a mask. The dress was made of fluffy pink and yellow feathers with longer plumes around the shoulders. The shoes and mask were red. The total effect, Cynthia thought, made Sheri look like a large pink-and-yellow chicken.

"Fabulous!" Ruth gasped.

"Scrumptious," added Cynthia as she swept the kitchen floor.

Sheri beamed. In a rare moment of magnanimity[7] she said to Cynthia, "I hope you don't feel bad about not going. It's just a silly dance."

"Oh, I know it is," Cynthia said, putting the broom in the closet and heading for the front door.

"Where are you going?" Ruth asked sharply.

"Uh, over to a friend's house to help him with his geography," Cynthia said.

"Well, just make sure you're home in time to walk Honey Plum," Ruth said.

Moments later Cynthia hurried through the night toward the address on Lexington Avenue Sam had given her. Most of the shops were closed and as Cynthia walked she imagined muggers lurching out of the dark shadows on the sidewalk. She was frightened by every move and sudden sound. Finally she came to a darkened storefront protected by a heavy iron gate. The sign above the gate said LEXINGTON THRIFT SHOP. In the window Cynthia could make out an old dresser, a black hat with a veil, and some dusty plates.

She heard the rapping of leather shoes against the pavement and spun around. A dark figure covered with a cape came toward her. Cynthia cowered.

"Lovely night, don't you think?" Sam pulled the hood off the cape.

7 **magnanimity:** generosity

Cynthia sighed with relief as Sam took out a set of keys and began undoing the locks on the iron gate. It squeaked and clattered as he pulled it up just high enough to duck underneath. Cynthia hesitated.

"Don't worry," Sam said. "My mother does volunteer work here three days a week. Just remember, whatever we borrow we must return."

Cynthia ducked under the gate and stepped into the darkened shop. It smelled musty like an old attic and was filled with furniture, kitchenware, and clothing.

"This way," Sam whispered, leading her through the dark. Cynthia almost tripped over a footstool. *"Careful!"*

She followed him down the stairs into the basement. Sam flicked on a light and Cynthia found herself in a room filled with oil paintings in gilt[8] frames, antique tables and chairs, and marble sculptures. Along one wall stood a rack of garment bags. Sam pulled one open and Cynthia gasped. Inside were beautiful old evening dresses.

Sam opened more bags. Inside were the most beautiful dresses Cynthia had ever seen. Some were made of satin, taffeta, and lace. Others had thick crinolines.[9] The dresses were old, but most were in almost perfect condition. "What are they doing here?" she asked.

"Donated years ago for tax write-offs," Sam said. "But the people who shop here have no use for stuff like this, so it sits around forever."

"Amazing." Cynthia gasped.

"No, rather sad actually," said Sam.

▲ ▲ ▲

On the afternoon of the cotillion Sheri left school early complaining of hot flashes. She spent the entire afternoon and evening primping in front of the mirror. Then, just before it was time to go, she decided her new red shoes were all wrong. For the next half hour she hopped around the apartment in her chicken outfit trying to find another pair with the right look and fit.

"Oh, it's hopeless!" she wailed. "The ones that look right don't fit and the ones that fit don't look right."

"Bergdorf's is open late," Ruth shouted. "If we hurry, we can make it!"

As mother and daughter rushed for the door, Ruth turned to Cynthia and said, "There's a frozen chicken pot pie in the refrigerator for dinner,

8 **gilt:** finished in gold
9 **crinolines:** full, stiff underskirts

darling. And don't forget to be a dear and clean the kitchen and walk Honey Plum."

As soon as the door closed Cynthia ran to the phone and called Sam's house. "They left."

"I'll be right over," Sam said.

▲   ▲   ▲

Sam arrived carrying a Val-Pak with Cynthia's dress inside. He was wearing a black tux with a white wing collar shirt. Instead of a bow tie he had on a western string tie, and he'd pulled his hair back into a ponytail. Cynthia blinked. With all the hair out of his face he was a good-looking guy.

"What is it?" Sam asked.

"Oh, nothing," Cynthia said, averting her gaze.

Sam took the dress out of the bag. It was strapless, made of shimmering red silk, with a long pleated skirt. Cynthia tried it on it the bathroom. She put her hair up, and applied Ruth's expensive makeup. Staring at herself in the mirror, she thought she looked good. Not spectacular, but certainly presentable.

Sam knocked on the bathroom door. "Come on, let's see."

Cynthia opened the door. Sam's eyes went wide and he clasped his hands. "You look wonderful, divine! God, what a beautiful neck you have!"

"I look okay," Cynthia corrected him.

"But wait," Sam said, reaching into the Val-Pak. "We're not through." He took out a black satin pouch and pulled something glittering out of it. Cynthia gasped. It was the most beautiful diamond-and-ruby necklace she'd ever seen.

"Where did you get it?" she asked, awestruck.

"It was lying around my mom's dresser," Sam said, reaching into the pouch again. "Here's the matching bracelet and earrings."

Cynthia held up the necklace and watched it shimmer in the bathroom light. The only place she'd ever seen jewelry like this was in magazines. "Is it real?"

"Be serious," Sam said. "Mom keeps her real jewels in a vault. These are just the best fakes money can buy."

It didn't matter. Cynthia put them on and gazed at herself in the mirror. Even she had to admit she looked grand.

"And don't forget this," Sam said, pulling a red, bejeweled mask out of the pouch.

Cynthia took the mask and held it up to her face. She looked like someone in a movie.

Sam glanced at his watch. "Now let's go!"

Cynthia pulled the mask from her face. "Wait. What about shoes?"

"Don't you have shoes?" Sam asked.

"No. I thought you were bringing them."

"Oh, God." Sam groaned.

They searched through Cynthia's closet, but all she had were sneakers and flats. Next they tried Ruth's closet, but her heels were too long. Finally they looked in Sheri's closet.

"What about these?" Sam asked, holding up the new red shoes. "The color's perfect."

Cynthia tried them on. "They're three sizes too big."

"Don't worry," Sam said. "We'll stuff the toes with newspaper."

A few moments later they were walking quickly toward Roper. Cynthia wore sneakers and carried the red shoes in a D'Agostino[10] shopping bag.

"I can't believe how nervous I am," she said.

"It's natural," Sam said.

"But I don't even like dances," she said.

"No one does."

"Then let's not go." Cynthia started to turn but Sam grabbed her arm.

"If we don't go," he said, deadly serious, "then the jerks who do will think they're better than us."

"So?"

"So tonight you show them," Sam said. "Then tomorrow you can tell them where to go."

She knew he was right. Half of her cared, and half of her didn't. But she was already dressed.

The Roper gymnasium was decorated with blue and pink balloons and streamers. A mirrored ball hanging from the ceiling sent stars sweeping across the costumed dancers as a loud band played. In the girls' room outside the gym Cynthia stuffed the toes of Sheri's shoes with tissue paper. Then she and Sam put on their masks and joined the crowd.

▲   ▲   ▲

That evening Cynthia danced with pirates, princes, policemen, and penguins. Her picture was taken for the school newspaper and yearbook. At

10 **D'Agostino:** a chain of grocery stores

one point she saw Sheri huddled with her friends, glancing at her and whispering. Behind her mask, her identity still unknown, she had become the object of jealousy. At Roper there was no higher form of flattery.

During a break at the punch table she giggled with Sam.

"You're the hit of the cotillion," he whispered. "Everyone's dying to find out who you are."

"They'll be disappointed," Cynthia whispered back.

Sam smiled and squeezed her hand. "I don't think so." They moved closer. . . .

Just then the band began to play again. Cynthia felt a finger tap on the shoulder. She turned and found a tall broad-shouldered boy in a Lone Ranger costume. Gazing into the steel-blue contact lenses behind the mask, she realized he was The One.

"Wanna dance?" he asked.

"Love to," she said.

The One danced divinely, sweeping her across the floor, twirling and spinning her gracefully. She loved the feeling of his arms around her, and the way the other dancers made room for them wherever their feet led.

"So can I see who's behind that mask?" The One asked between dances.

"That depends," she replied.

"Oh, I get it," The One said.

The band started playing a slow song and The One gathered her into his arms. "I'm getting a red BMW convertible for my eighteenth birthday," he told her.

"Wonderful," Cynthia said. "I've never ridden in one."

"My family has a house in Virgin Gorda,"[11] he said.

"I hear it's beautiful there," said Cynthia.

"My grandfather just donated a laboratory to Brown,"[12] The One said. "I've only got a C average, but I'm a shoo-in."

"Great school," said Cynthia.

The song ended. "Is it time to see who you are?" The One asked.

Time, Cynthia thought. Suddenly she looked at her watch. It was ten forty-eight. In twelve minutes Honey Plum was going to drench the Persian rug! Cynthia dashed out of the dance. Behind her she heard The One shout for her to wait, but there was no time to explain. As she ran,

11 **Virgin Gorda:** one of the Virgin Isands in the West Indies

12 **Brown:** Brown University is an exclusive university in Providence, Rhode Island.

one of her shoes flew off, but she didn't stop to retrieve it. In the girls' room she threw on her sneakers. A moment later she was sprinting toward Park Avenue.

The grandfather clock was tolling eleven as she let herself into the apartment. In the living room Honey Plum was lifting his leg. Cynthia grabbed the leash and managed to drag him outside just in time.

▲　▲　▲

On Monday the school was abuzz about the mystery girl in the red gown. Who was she? Where had she come from? Where had she gone? At lunch Sam slid his tray next to hers. "You won't believe this," he whispered, "but The One is going around school with your shoe asking every girl to try it on. He swears he's madly in love and has to find the owner."

No sooner had he said it than The One appeared in front of them with the red shoe. He gazed deeply into her eyes and she felt goose bumps rise on her arms. A crowd formed around the table.

"Were you at the dance?" The One asked.

"Yes," Cynthia said.

"Did you wear a red gown?"

"Yes."

"And jewelry?

"Yes."

The One looked down at her feet and then back into her eyes. "Would you try this shoe on?"

"Yes." Cynthia slipped off her sneaker and The One slid the shoe on.

"It fits!" he cried. The crowd around them gasped.

As Conner Worthington Harkness the Third reached up for her hand, Cynthia glanced at Sam. For a split second he looked heartbroken. Then he managed a brave smile. Even in his pain he was happy for her. Cynthia looked back down at The One, who was now on his knees.

"I can't believe I found you," he said. "I want you to ride in my BMW. I want you to fly with me to Virgin Gorda. I'll ask my grandfather to donate another lab to Brown so you can go there too."

Sam started to get up. Cynthia watched him slide his tray away from hers. He had been her friend when no one else was interested. He had given her the gown and the jewels. More than that, he'd given her the courage to go to the dance.

"Wait," Cynthia said, sliding the shoe off and pulling out the tissue paper. "Someone stuffed paper in the toe. See? It really doesn't fit me at all."

The One took the shoe back. "Then who . . . ?"

"Come to think of it," Cynthia said, "it looks just like my stepsister Sheri's shoe. Why don't you try her?"

Scowling, The One stood up and went off in search of Sheri. The crowd followed him, leaving Cynthia and Sam alone.

Sam looked stunned. " But he's The One."

Cynthia smiled and put her arm around his shoulder. "Not for me he isn't." ❧

Side 32

VICTOR HERNÁNDEZ CRUZ

I am glad that I am not one of those
Big Con Edison[1] pipes that sits by the
River crying smoke
I am glad I am not the doorknob
Of a police car patrolling the Lower
East Side[2]
How cool I am not a subway token
That has been lost and is sitting
Quietly and lonely by the edge of
A building on 47th Street
I am nothing and no one
I am the possibility of everything
I am a man in this crazy city
I am a door and a glass of water
I am a guitar string cutting through the
Smog
Vibrating and bringing morning
My head is a butterfly
Over the traffic jams

1 **Con Edison:** the company
  that supplies New York
  City with electricity

2 **Lower East Side:** lively
  neighborhood in New
  York City

EAST RIVER FROM THE SHELTON
1927-28
Georgia O'Keeffe

New Jersey State Museum Collection

Fox Hunt

LENSEY NAMIOKA

Andy Liang watched the kids from his school bus walk home with their friends. He could hear them talking together and laughing. He always got off the bus alone and walked home by himself.

But this time it was different. A girl got off the bus just behind him and started walking in the same direction. He wondered why he hadn't seen her before. She was also Asian American, which made it all the more surprising that he hadn't noticed her earlier.

As he tried to get a better look, she went into the neighborhood convenience store and disappeared behind a shelf of canned soup. He peered into the store, hoping for another glimpse of her. All he saw were some of the kids from the bus getting bags of potato chips and soft drinks.

Andy sighed. He was used to being a loner, and usually it didn't bother him—not much, anyway. But today the loneliness was heavy. He overheard the other kids talking, and he knew they were planning to study together for the PSAT.[1] From the looks of the snacks, they were expecting a long session.

Andy would be practicing for the test, too, but he would be doing it by himself. *I'm better off doing it alone, anyway,* he thought. *Studying with somebody else would just slow me down.*

The truth was that none of the others had invited him to study with them. *So all right,* he said to himself, *they think I'm a grind.[2] What's wrong*

---

1 **PSAT:** an abbreviation for the Preliminary Scholastic Aptitude Test, a practice test for the SAT, a college admission examination

2 **grind:** slang for a person who is focused on academics

with that? I'll be getting better scores on the PSAT than any of them, even if there's nobody to coach me.

He finally found the girl standing in front of a case of barbecued chicken. She was staring so hungrily at the chickens that his own mouth began watering, and he would have bought a piece on the spot if he had the money. But with the change in his pocket, he had to be satisfied with a candy bar.

Leaving the store, he reached his street and passed the corner house with the moody German shepherd. As usual, it snapped at him, and he automatically retreated to the far side of the sidewalk. Although the dog was on a chain, Andy didn't like the way it looked at him. Besides, a chain could always break.

Today, the dog not only snapped, it began to bark furiously and strained against its chain. Andy jumped back and bumped against the girl he had seen earlier. Somehow she had appeared behind him without making any noise.

He apologized. "I didn't mean to crash into you. That dog always growls at me, but today he's really barking like crazy."

The girl shivered. "The dog doesn't seem to like me very much, either." Before he had a chance to say anything more, she turned and walked away.

Again Andy sighed. He hadn't even had a chance to find out what her name was or where she lived. Was she Chinese American, as he was? What grade was she in? At least she went on the same school bus, so there was a chance of seeing her again.

But he didn't have much hope that she would be interested in him. Girls didn't go for the quiet, studious type. Last year, one of the girls in his geometry class had asked him to give her some help

after school. That went pretty well, and for a while he thought they might have something going. But after she passed the geometry test, she didn't look at him again.

Maybe if he studied less and went in for sports, girls would get interested in him. But then his grades might slip, and his parents would never let him hear the end of it. He had to keep his grades up, study hard, be the dutiful son.

His brother had managed to get a math score of 800 on the PSAT, and now he was at Yale with a full scholarship. Andy had to try and do as well.

More than once he had asked his parents why it was so important to get into a good college. "Lots of people get rich in this country without going to college at all," he told them.

His father would draw himself up stiffly. "The Liangs belonged to the mandarin[3] class in China. I've told you again and again that to become a mandarin, one had to pass the official examinations. Only outstanding scholars passed, and only they had the qualifications to govern the country."

Andy's father always got worked up about the subject. He might be only a minor clerk in America, he said, but he was descended from a family of high-ranking officials in China.

Another thing Andy noticed was that when his father went on at length about the illustrious Liang family, his mother always listened with a faint smile. She seemed to be amused for some reason.

But that didn't stop her from also putting pressure on Andy to study hard. Every night, she would ask him whether he had done his homework, and she double-checked his papers to make sure everything was correct.

Normally Andy didn't mind doing his homework. He liked the satisfaction of a job well done when he finished a hard problem in math. But lately, all the extra work preparing for the exam was beginning to get him down. His mind wandered, and he began to daydream. He had visions of becoming a snake charmer, making a balloon trip over the Andes, or practicing kung fu in Shaolin Temple.[4] He saw himself in the English countryside, riding a galloping horse in a fox hunt.

He tried to stop wasting time on these stupid daydreams. Maybe his mind wouldn't wander if he had someone to study with. But nobody wanted to study with him. Nobody wanted to spend time with a nerd.

---

3 **mandarin:** aristocratic

4 **Shaolin Temple:** a Buddhist temple in north central China

▲ ▲ ▲

Next day, the girl got off the bus again with Andy, and this time, instead of going into the convenience store, she began to walk with him. When they reached the yard with the German shepherd, they both automatically backed away from the fence.

Andy and the girl looked at each other and grinned. He was encouraged. "I'm Andy Liang. Are you new in the neighborhood?"

"We moved here last week," she replied. "My name is Leona Hu. But Leona is a silly name, and my friends call me Lee."

She was inviting him to call her Lee and including him among her friends! Andy could hardly believe his luck. An attractive girl was actually ready to be friends. He was grateful to the German shepherd.

The girl had big almond-shaped eyes. Andy had overheard Americans saying that Chinese had slanty eyes, although his own eyes did not slant. Lee's eyes, on the other hand, definitely slanted upward at the corners.

Her hair had a slightly reddish tint, instead of being blue-black like his own. She wasn't exactly beautiful, but with her hair and her slanting eyes, she looked exotic and fascinating.

When they came to his house, Andy wished he could keep Lee talking with him. But she smiled at him briefly and went on. He had to stop himself from running after her to find out where she lived. He didn't want her to think that he was pestering her.

Was she going to take the PSAT this year? If she was, maybe they could study together!

▲ ▲ ▲

At dinner that night, his father went on as usual about how important it was to do well on the PSAT. "We immigrants start at the bottom here in America, and the only way we can pull ourselves up is to get a good education. Never forget that you're descended from illustrious ancestors, Andy."

Again, Andy noticed his mother's faint smile. Later, he went into the kitchen where he found her washing the dishes. "Why do you always smile when Father gives me his pep talk about education? Don't you agree with him?"

"Oh, I agree with him about the importance of education," his mother said. "I'm just amused by all that talk about *illustrious ancestors.*"

"You mean Father wasn't telling the truth about Liangs being mandarins?" asked Andy. He took up a bunch of chopsticks and began to wipe them dry. Usually, his mother refused his help with the chores. She wanted him to spend all his time on his homework.

But tonight she didn't immediately send him upstairs to his desk. She rinsed a rice bowl and put it in the dish rack. "Well, the Liangs haven't always been mandarins," she said finally. "They used to be quite poor, until one of them achieved success by passing the official examinations and raising the status of the whole Liang family."

"Hey, that's great!" Andy liked the idea of a poor boy making good. It was more interesting than coming from a long line of decadent aristocrats. "Tell me more about this ancestor."

"His name was Fujin Liang," replied his mother. "Or I should say Liang Fujin, since in China, last names come first." Again she smiled faintly. "Very well. You should really be studying, but it's good for you to know about your ancestors."

▲　▲　▲

Liang Fujin lived with his widowed mother in a small thatched cottage and earned money by looking after a neighbor's water buffalo. His mother added to their meager income by weaving and selling cotton cloth. It was a hard struggle to put rice in their bowls.

But Fujin's mother was ambitious for him. She knew he was smart, and she decided that he should try for the official examinations. In theory, any poor boy could take the examinations, and if he passed, he could raise his family to mandarin status. But rich boys could afford tutors to help them study. For Fujin, even buying a book was a luxury.

He was so eager to learn that he crouched under the window of the nearby school and tried to eavesdrop on the lessons. Whenever he saved enough money to buy books, he would read them while seated on the back of the water buffalo. Once he was so absorbed that he walked the buffalo into a rice paddy. But he managed to read the precious books until he knew them all by heart.

Through hard work he grew up to be a fine scholar. His mother thought he was finally ready to take the examinations, but he himself wasn't so confident. The other competitors were the sons of rich families, who could afford the very best tutors.

He continued to study late every night, until his head began to nod. So he tied the end of his pigtail to a nail in the ceiling, and whenever his head fell forward, the pigtail jerked him awake.

One night, while he was struggling to stay awake over his book, he heard a soft voice behind him. "A fine, hardworking young man like you deserves to pass the examination."

Fujin whirled around and saw a beautiful girl standing behind him. Somehow she had appeared without making any noise. She had huge, bewitching eyes that slanted sharply. Could he be dreaming?

"Let me help you," continued the girl. "I can act as a tutor and coach you."

▲   ▲   ▲

"And that was how your ancestor, Liang Fujin, got the coaching he needed to pass the examinations," said Andy's mother.

Andy blinked. "But . . . but who was this mysterious girl? And how come she was such a great scholar? I thought women didn't get much education in the old days."

His mother laughed. "Nobody in the Liang family would say. But I'll give you a hint: When the girl lifted her skirt to sit down, Fujin caught a flash of something swishing. It looked like a long, bushy tail!"

It took Andy a moment to get it. Then he remembered the Chinese stories his mother used to tell him, stories about the *huli jing,* or fox spirit. The mischievous fox, or *huli,* often appeared in the form of a beautiful girl and played tricks on people. But in some of the stories, the fox fell in love with a handsome young man and did him a great service. She expected a reward for her service, of course, and the reward was marriage.

"So my ancestor passed the examinations because he was coached by a fox?" asked Andy.

"That story is a lie!" cried Andy's father, stomping into the kitchen. "It was made up by malicious neighbors who were jealous of the Liangs!"

Andy's mother shrugged and began to pack the dishes away. His father continued. "Liang Fujin passed the examinations because he was smart and worked hard! Don't you forget it, Andy! So now you can go up to your room and start working!"

His father was right, of course. Fox spirits belonged in fairy tales. He, Andy Liang, would have to study for the PSAT the hard way.

▲   ▲   ▲

Andy was delighted when Lee told him that she was also planning to take the PSAT. She agreed that it would be a good idea to study together. He was eager to begin that very evening. "How about coming over to my house? I'm sure my parents would love to meet you."

Actually, he wasn't sure how delighted his parents would be. He suspected that they would be glad to see him with a Chinese American girl, but they'd probably think that a girl—any girl—would distract him from his studies.

He was half sorry and half relieved when she said, "I'm going to be busy tonight. Maybe we can go to the public library tomorrow afternoon and get some sample tests and study guides."

That night he had a dream about fox hunting. Only this time, he found himself running on the ground trying to get away from the mounted horsemen and howling dogs. There was somebody running with him—another fox, with reddish hair and a bushy tail. It flashed a look at him with its slanting eyes.

▲ ▲ ▲

Andy and Lee began studying sample PSAT tests at the library. Working with someone else certainly made studying less of a drudgery. Andy felt relaxed with Lee. He didn't suffer the paralyzing shyness with her that seized him when he was with other girls.

She was really good at finding out what his weaknesses were. English grammar was his worst subject, and Lee fed him the right questions so that the fuzzy points of grammar got cleared up. As the days went by, Andy became confident that he was going to do really well on the PSAT. At this rate, he might get a scholarship to some famous university.

Chinese stick puppet.

He began to worry that the help was one-sided. *He* was getting first-rate coaching, but what was Lee getting out of this? "You're helping me so much," he told her. "But I don't see how I'm helping you at all."

She smiled at him. "I'll get my reward someday."

Something about her glance looked familiar. Where had he seen it before?

▲ ▲ ▲

They had an extralong study session the day before the exam. When they passed the corner house on their way home, the German shepherd went into a frenzy of barking and scrabbled to climb the Cyclone fence. Both the chain and the fence held, fortunately. Lee looked shaken and backed away from the fence.

At Andy's house she recovered her color. "Well, good luck on the exam tomorrow." She looked at him for a moment with her slanting eyes, and then she was gone.

Again, he thought he remembered that look from somewhere. All during supper, he was tantalized by the memory, which was just out of reach.

That night he dreamed about fox hunting again. It was more vivid than usual, and he could see the scarlet coats of the riders chasing him. The howling of the dogs sounded just like the German shepherd. Again, he was running with another fox. It had huge slanting eyes, bright with mischief.

He woke up, and as he sat in his bed, he finally remembered where he had seen those huge, slanting eyes. They were Lee's eyes.

Next day Andy met Lee at the entrance to the examination hall. He suddenly realized that if he said her name in the Chinese order, it would be Hu Lee, which sounded the same as *huli,* or fox.

She smiled. "So you know?"

Andy found his voice. "Why did you pick me, particularly?"

Her smile widened. "We foxes hunt out our own kind."

That was when Andy knew why the German shepherd always snapped at him. He himself must be part fox. His ancestor, Liang Fujin, had accepted help from the fox spirit after all, and she had collected her reward. ∾

Holly, age fifteen

AS TOLD TO JILL KREMENTZ

At about one-thirty in the afternoon, the telephone rang, and the voice on the other end asked for my mother. It was a Saturday and I was home alone. I said she was out, so the caller asked me to write down her name, address, and telephone number, which I did. Then the woman who was on the other end of the phone said, "Fourteen years ago I had a baby that I gave up for adoption. I believe you are my daughter."

I was in total shock, and as we talked, my mind was in a different world. She asked me a lot of questions about myself and filled me in on what had happened to her. She said she was five-foot-four, had blond hair and green eyes, and that she worked for a management consulting company. And she explained why she had put me up for adoption. She was seventeen when she met and fell in love with my birthfather, but by the time she found out she was pregnant they had broken up. She wanted to keep me, but her mother talked her out of it. She told me she had gotten married since then, to someone else, but was presently divorced and she didn't have any other kids. We talked for about an hour, and after I hung up I started sobbing. One of my father's friends, Mike Rodgers, came in the door looking for my parents, and I put my arms around him and just kept on crying and crying. I couldn't stop.

I wasn't crying because I was sad. I had planned on searching when I got a little older, and my parents were going to help me. In fact, it was something we had talked about very recently. So I was happy that my birthmother had found me, but I never expected it to be so all-of-a-sudden. I always figured I had till tomorrow—you know, a few years more before I really had to deal with it.

I was finally able to tell Mike about the phone call, and he drove me over to where my mother—my adoptive mother—was working. On the way over we met my Dad, but I was still crying so hard I couldn't explain what had happened—I couldn't get the words out of my mouth. He thought someone had died until I was finally able to tell him, and then he didn't know what to say. I had to leave for a basketball game at school, so he went and picked up Mom at work, told her to sit down, and told her everything. When I got home from the game, we all talked and decided it would be best to begin a relationship slowly—that we would just exchange information and photographs by mail for a while. That's what we did for about two months. I was still wandering around in a daze during this time, and I was worried about how my life might change. My mother said I should just think of Alison, my birthmother, as a friend, and that I should try to put myself in her position, so that's what I tried to do. And then in May we finally met. We invited Alison to stay with us for a few days, and she flew out for a weekend visit. My parents and I met her at the airport, and that was really weird. I was glad we were a little bit late because that gave us something to talk about while we were walking through the terminal. After we got to our house she gave me a picture of my birthfather and also the little bracelet they had put on my wrist when I was born. She had kept it all these years.

We spent the weekend mostly talking about what she had been doing since I was born and how she had found me. It took her eight months and a lot of work, calling around and checking records. I showed her my scrapbook and told her about my school—stuff like that. We didn't go out anywhere, and I didn't get a chance to introduce her to any of my friends. We had a good visit, and after she left, we wrote letters back and forth.

The following month, after school got out, I went to visit her for a week. That was really exciting because I had never been to New York before, but it upset me when her friends would say stuff like "So you're Alison's daughter." I didn't know what to say. I sort of went along with it because I didn't know what else they could call me, but by not saying anything, I felt like I was taking away something from my Mom. It's confusing because I don't know how to categorize my relationship with Alison. I don't want to think of it as purely biological, but I don't know how else to define it. I feel ridiculous introducing her as "my friend," and yet I certainly don't think of her as my mother. Nor do I want to. In my view I have only one mother and that's the mother who raised me and mothered me—who gave me food and shelter and love while I was grow-ing up. That's my definition of a mother. My birthmother's the person who gave me my heredity and my life, and while I don't want to push her away, I also don't want to take anything away from my Mom. I don't want my mother to feel any loss of prestige.

One thing that's nice about Alison—it's a part of her that I really enjoy—is that she loves to do new things like ice-skating or trying new restaurants. My Mom, who isn't particularly adventurous, says this is good for me. She wants me to have new experiences and grow as a per-son. I know she probably feels a little threatened by Alison, who's ten years younger than she is, but I think she's so secure about herself as a person that she can handle it. And since I tend to be somewhat shy, it has been great for me to travel a little and spread my wings. Still, I pre-fer having Alison visit us. She flew down again this Easter for a week, and I felt much more comfortable and secure in my own environment. Last winter, when I went to see her, I felt my parents were trying to push me away. I know they were just trying to be nice and let me know I was free to visit her for however long I wanted—that it wouldn't hurt their feelings or make them feel rejected—but instead of making me feel free, it made me worry that they didn't love me, that they were rejecting me!

The past two years have been real hard on my parents. I get the feeling that sometimes they're thinking that they're losing me, and that's the last thing in the world I want them to feel. It isn't true. And most of all, I don't want to lose them. Once, when my mother and I were having a fight—the way all mothers and daughters have arguments—my Mom said something like "Well, you can just go and live with Alison." Even though I knew she didn't mean it, I felt really hurt. That's the sort of thing that can't ever be said—not in the heat of an argument, and not even joking around.

I think I'm probably mature for my age, so I've been able to handle all of this fairly well. But that initial phone call was definitely a bad idea. If I was a birthmother and I had a fourteen-year-old daughter, I'd probably go through her parents first. And if I was scared that her parents wouldn't let me talk to her, or possibly wouldn't even tell me I'd called and would just send me a lawyer's letter telling me to get lost, then I'd try to use an intermediary.[1] Calling directly is just too big a shock for a kid. The whole notion of searching is still pretty new, and it's hard for anyone to know how to act, so I'm not mad at Alison and I *am* glad she found me. That's

1 **intermediary:** a go-between

all in the past. Right now we have to deal with the future, and my main concern is that Alison may expect more out of me than I can give. It would be sad if she wanted to make me the center of her existence, because I can't do the same thing for her. I want to be friendly but I don't want anything past that. I know where she is and what she looks like, and that's great, but it's all I ever wanted or needed.

Alison and I have talked about this and she told me I don't need to worry—that any relationship is determined by mutual consent.[2] She says all she wants is for us to be honest and open with each other, and no matter what happens, just knowing that I'm alive and well is wonderful for her. I hope that's true because right now I'm feeling real protective about my Mom and I'd hate to feel I have two mothers. I'd like to keep in touch with Alison, but anything beyond that is too much of a responsibility for me. We've each got our own life to live. ∾

Holly.

2 **mutual consent:** agreement between two or more people

Birthday Box

JANE YOLEN

I was ten years old when my mother died. Ten years old on that very day. Still she gave me a party of sorts. Sick as she was, Mama had seen to it, organizing it at the hospital. She made sure the doctors and nurses all brought me presents. We were good friends with them all by that time, because Mama had been in the hospital for so long.

The head nurse, V. Louise Higgins (I never did know what that *V* stood for), gave me a little box, which was sort of funny because she was the biggest of all the nurses there. I mean she was tremendous. And she was the only one who insisted on wearing all white. Mama had called her the great white shark when she was first admitted, only not to V. Louise's face. "All those needles," Mama had said. "Like teeth." But V. Louise was sweet, not sharklike at all, and she'd been so gentle with Mama.

I opened the little present first. It was a fountain pen, a real one, not a fake one like you get at Kmart.

"Now you can write beautiful stories, Katie," V. Louise said to me.

I didn't say that stories come out of your head, not out of a pen. That wouldn't have been polite, and Mama—even sick—was real big on politeness.

"Thanks, V. Louise," I said.

The Stardust Twins—which is what Mama called Patty and Tracey-lynn because they reminded her of dancers in an old-fashioned ballroom— gave me a present together. It was a diary and had a picture of a little girl in pink, reading in a garden swing. A little young for me, a little too cute. I mean, I read Stephen King and want to write like him. But as Mama always reminded me whenever Dad finally remembered to send me something, it was the thought that counted, not the actual gift.

"It's great," I told them. "I'll write in it with my new pen." And I wrote my name on the first page just to show them I meant it.

They hugged me and winked at Mama. She tried to wink back but was just too tired and shut both her eyes instead.

Lily, who is from Jamaica, had baked me some sweet bread. Mary Margaret gave me a gold cross blessed by the pope, which I put on even though Mama and I weren't churchgoers. That was Dad's thing.

Then Dr. Dann, the intern who was on days, and Dr. Pucci, the oncologist (which is the fancy name for a cancer doctor), gave me a big box filled to the top with little presents, each wrapped up individually. All things they knew I'd love—paperback books and writing paper and erasers with funny animal heads and colored paper clips and a rubber stamp that printed FROM KATIE'S DESK and other stuff. They must have raided a stationery store.

There was one box, though, they held out till the end. It was about the size of a large top hat. The paper was deep blue and covered with stars; not fake stars but real stars, I mean, like a map of the night sky. The ribbon was two shades of blue with silver threads running through. There was no name on the card.

"Who's it from?" I asked.

None of the nurses answered, and the doctors both suddenly were studying the ceiling tiles with the kind of intensity they usually saved for X rays. No one spoke. In fact the only sound for the longest time was Mama's breathing machine going in and out and in and out. It was a harsh, horrible, insistent sound, and usually I talked and talked to cover up the noise. But I was waiting for someone to tell me.

At last V. Louise said, "It's from your mama, Katie. She told us what she wanted. And where to get it."

I turned and looked at Mama then, and her eyes were open again. Funny, but sickness had made her even more beautiful than good health had. Her skin was like that old paper, the kind they used to write on with quill pens, and stretched out over her bones so she looked like a model. Her eyes, which had been a deep, brilliant blue, were now like the fall sky, bleached and softened. She was like a faded photograph of herself. She smiled a very small smile at me. I knew it was an effort.

"It's you," she mouthed. I read her lips. I had gotten real good at that. I thought she meant it was a present for me.

"Of course it is," I said cheerfully. I had gotten good at that, too, being cheerful when I didn't feel like it. "Of course it is."

I took the paper off the box carefully, not tearing it but folding it into a tidy packet. I twisted the ribbons around my hand and then put them on the pillow by her hand. It made the stark white hospital bed look almost festive.

Under the wrapping, the box was beautiful itself. It was made of a heavy cardboard and covered with a linen material that had a pattern of cloud-filled skies.

I opened the box slowly and . . .

"It's empty," I said. "Is this a joke?" I turned to ask Mama, but she was gone. I mean, her body was there, but she wasn't. It was as if she was as empty as the box.

Dr. Pucci leaned over her and listened with a stethoscope, then almost absently patted Mama's head. Then, with infinite care, V. Louise closed Mama's eyes, ran her hand across Mama's cheek, and turned off the breathing machine.

"Mama!" I cried. And to the nurses and doctors, I screamed, "Do something!" And because the room had suddenly become so silent, my voice echoed back at me. "Mama, do something."

▲ ▲ ▲

I cried steadily for, I think, a week. Then I cried at night for a couple of months. And then for about a year I cried at anniversaries, like Mama's birthday or mine, at Thanksgiving, on Mother's Day. I stopped writing. I stopped reading except for school assignments. I was pretty mean to my half brothers and totally rotten to my stepmother and Dad. I felt empty and angry, and they all left me pretty much alone.

And then one night, right after my first birthday without Mama, I woke up remembering how she had said, "It's you." Not, "It's for you," just "It's you." Now Mama had been a high school English teacher and a writer herself. She'd had poems published in little magazines. She didn't use words carelessly. In the end she could hardly use any words at all. So—I asked myself in that dark room—why had she said, "It's you"? Why were they the very last words she had ever said to me, forced out with her last breath?

I turned on the bedside light and got out of bed. The room was full of shadows, not all of them real.

Pulling the desk chair over to my closet, I climbed up and felt along the top shelf, and against the back wall, there was the birthday box, just where I had thrown it the day I had moved in with my dad.

I pulled it down and opened it. It was as empty as the day I had put it away.

"It's you," I whispered to the box.

And then suddenly I knew.

Mama had meant *I* was the box, solid and sturdy, maybe even beautiful or at least interesting on the outside. But I had to fill up the box to make it all it could be. And I had to fill me up as well. She had guessed what might happen to me, had told me in a subtle way. In the two words she could manage.

I stopped crying and got some paper out of the desk drawer. I got out my fountain pen. I started writing, and I haven't stopped since. The first thing I wrote was about that birthday. I put it in the box, and pretty soon that box was overflowing with stories. And poems. And memories.

And so was I.

And so was I. ∾

RESPONDING TO CLUSTER FOUR

Thinking Skill   SYNTHESIZING

1. Each of the other clusters in this book is introduced by a question that is meant to help readers focus their thinking about the selections. What do you think the question for cluster four should be?

2. How do you think the selections in this cluster should be taught? Demonstrate your ideas by joining with your classmates to do one or more of the following.

   a. create discussion questions

   b. lead discussions about the selections

   c. develop vocabulary activities

   d. prepare a cluster quiz

REFLECTING ON *WHO AM I?*

Essential Question   WHO'S THE REAL YOU?

Reflecting on this book as a whole provides an opportunity for independent learning and the application of the critical thinking skill, synthesis. *Synthesizing* means examining all the things you have learned from this book and combining them to form a richer and more meaningful view of how we learn who we are.

There are many ways to demonstrate what you know about yourself. Here are some possibilities. Your teacher may provide others.

1. Answer the following question using what you have read and your own experience: How can you stay true to your own self when others try to change you? Provide examples to support your ideas.

2. Individually or in small groups, develop an independent project that demonstrates your feelings about your identity. For example, you might give a presentation on how you see yourself compared to how friends, family members, and teachers see you. Other options might include a music video, dance, poem, performance, drama, or artistic rendering.

ACKNOWLEDGMENTS

Text Credits CONTINUED FROM PAGE 2 "Fairy Tale" by Todd Strasser. Copyright © 1989 by Todd Strasser. Originally published in the collection *Connections*, edited by Donald R. Gallo (Delacorte Press). Reprinted by permission of the author.

"Fox Hunt," copyright © 1993 by Lensey Namioka, from *Join In: Multi-Ethnic Short Stories by Outstanding Writers for Young Adults*, edited by Donald R. Gallo. Reprinted by permission of Lensey Namioka. All rights are reserved by the Author.

"Getting Ready" by Debra Marquart, from *Everything's a Verb*. Minneapolis, Minnesota: New Rivers Press, 1995. Used by permission of the author.

"The Green Killer" by M. E. Kerr. Copyright © 1995 by M. E. Kerr. Reprinted by permission of the author.

"Holly, age fifteen" from *How It Feels To Be Adopted* by Jill Krementz. Copyright © 1982 by Jill Krementz. Reprinted by permission of Alfred A. Knopf, Inc.

"I'm Nobody!" or poem 288 from *The Poems of Emily Dickinson*, Thomas H. Johnson, ed., Cambridge, Massachusetts: The Belknap Press of Harvard University Press. Copyright © 1951, 1955, 1979, 1983 by the President and Fellows of Harvard College. Reprinted by permission of the publishers and the Trustees of Amherst College.

"Moon" from *Zebra and Other Stories* by Chaim Potok. Copyright © 1998 by Chaim Potok. Reprinted by permission of Alfred A. Knopf, Inc.

"On Being Seventeen, Bright, and Unable to Read" by David Raymond. Originally published in *The New York Times*, April 25, 1976. Copyright © 1976 by The New York Times Co. Reprinted by permission.

"Remember Me" from *Curses, Inc.* by Vivian Vande Velde, copyright © 1997 by Vivian Vande Velde, reprinted by permission of Harcourt, Inc.

"Saying Yes" by Diana Chang. Copyright © 1984 by Diana Chang. Reprinted by permission of the author.

"Side 32" from *Tropicalization* by Victor Hernández Cruz. Copyright © 1976 by Victor Hernández Cruz. Reprinted by permission of the author.

"Tiffany" from *Sugar in the Raw: Voices of Young Black Girls in America* by Rebecca Carroll. Copyright © 1997 by Rebecca Carroll. Reprinted by the permission of Clarkson N. Potter, a division of Crown Publishers, Inc.

"The Way Up" by William Hoffman. Copyright © 1966 by William Hoffman. First appeared in *Scholastic Teacher*, May 6, 1966 issue. Reprinted by permission of Curtis Brown, Ltd.

"Your Body Is Your ID" by Hank Schlesinger. Published in the January 1999 issue of *Popular Science*. Reprinted with permission from Popular Science Magazine, copyright © 1999, Times Mirror Magazines, Inc. Distributed by Los Angeles Times Syndicate.

Every reasonable effort has been made to properly acknowledge ownership of all material used. Any omissions or mistakes are not intentional and, if brought to the publisher's attention, will be corrected in future editions.

Photo and Art Credits Cover and Title Page: Milton Avery, *Seated Girl with Dog*, 1944. 44 x 32 inches, Roy R. Neuberger Collection. ©1999 Milton Avery Trust/Artists Rights Society (ARS), New York. Pages 4-5: © SPL/SPL/Photonica. Pages 11: Saul Steinberg, *Untitled Drawing*, 1953. ©1999 Estate of Saul Steinberg/Artists Rights Society (ARS), New York. Pages 12 and 23: Brian Cronin. Pages 25: ©1999 Lorna Clark/Photonica. Page 28: © Tommy Flynn/Photonica. Pages 30-31: Andrew Grivas and Alex Reardon. Page 34: ©Steven Edison/Photonica. Pages 40-41: © Mark E. Nelson/Photonica. Page 45: Calef Brown. Page 46: Duane Michals, *Who Am I?* Page 49: Fritz Winold Reiss, *Harlem Girl, I*, ca 1925. Pencil, charcoal and pastel on illustration board. Gift of Mr. W. Tjark Reiss, Museum of Art and Archaeology, University of Missouri-Columbia. Page 52: William Burlingham. Page 58: University of Colorado Museum, Cat. No. 33123. Page 62: Ray Dean/Photonica. Page 73: Ryan D. Li. Page 75: Ben Shahn, © Estate of Ben Shahn/Licensed by VAGA, New York, NY. Page 76: © Brian Wilson/Photonica. Page 88: © Remi Benali and Stephen Ferry/Liaison Agency. Page 91: Vivienne Flesher. Page 97: © John Van Hasselt/Sygma. Page 109: Tim Flach/Tony Stone Images. Page 111: Pierre Pratt. Page 112: © SPL/SPL/Photonica. 123: © Cheryl Koralik/Photonica. Page 125: Georgia O'Keeffe, *East River from the Shelton*. (1927-28). Oil on canvas, 27 1/16 x 21 15/16 inches. Purchased by the Friends of the New Jersey State Museum with a gift from Mary Lea Johnson. FA1972.229. Page 127: © Esbin/Anderson/Omni-Photo Communications. Page 132: Shadow puppet, leather, 11 1/2 inches high. Shanxi Provence, China. From *Chinese Folk Arts* by Nancy Zeng Berliner, New York Graphic Society published by Little, Brown & Company, 1986. Page 137: From *How It Feels to be Adopted* by Jill Krementz. Copyright ©1982 by Jill Krementz. Reprinted by permission of Alfred A. Knopf, Inc., a Divison of Random House, Inc. Page 138: William Burlingham.